INFORMATION AND COMMUNICATION
TECHNOLOGY
AND THE MANAGEMENT OF SCHOOLS IN
NIGERIA

REV. SR. OGOCHUKWU HONORATA NWOSU

WESTBOW
PRESS®
A DIVISION OF THOMAS NELSON
& ZONDERVAN

WestBow Press books may be ordered through booksellers or by contacting:

WestBow Press
A Division of Thomas Nelson & Zondervan
1663 Liberty Drive
Bloomington, IN 47403
www.westbowpress.com
844-714-3454

ISBN: 978-1-6642-1000-4 (sc)
ISBN: 978-1-6642-1002-8 (hc)
ISBN: 978-1-6642-1001-1 (e)

Library of Congress Control Number: 2020921130

Print information available on the last page.

WestBow Press rev. date: 10/28/2020

CONTENTS

FOREWORD

My favourite matrass is that good mentors are difficult to find so also authentic mentees, especially from the opposite sex, are hard to discover. Mentoring the author of this book throughout her PhD programme and till now was initially a hard choice but finally turned out to be a rewarding experience by God's grace. A hard choice because she was neither my student nor from my university when we met. With time, Rev. Sr. Ogochukwu Honorata Nwosu (PhD) demonstrated high integrity, maturity, perseverance, temperance, intrinsic motivation and respect for boundaries in professional relationship. She proved to be highly trustworthy. In fact, it is a great privilege to write the preface to this book on "Information and Communication Technology and the Management of Schools in Nigeria".

The book is a timely subject of discussion across the world in an era when synergy among scientific knowledge, technology and education is preached as a solution to many socioeconomic ills. Chapter one focused on various concepts of Information, Communication and Technologies (ICT) with emphasis on the meaning, the components, characteristics, types, importance and its application in education. Chapter two discussed ICT integration and deployment in planning, staffing, directing, motivating, monitoring, controlling and coordinating staff, students and other education resources. Chapter two also focused on ICT tools such as e-learning, blended learning, open and distance learning, video conferencing, and Interactive Radio Counseling. Chapter three to five logically and specifically discussed issues relating to the deployment of ICT at the primary, secondary and tertiary levels of education respectively. I believe the book would provide the needed information for both students and practitioners in Educational Management Information System (EMIS).

I therefore, commend this book to students and staff of education, knowledge management and educational management.

Professor Joel Babatunde Babalola, FNAEAP

DEDICATION

This book is dedicated to the Almighty God for the inspiration to put these things down.

ACKNOWLEDGMENT

Most of all, my unending gratitude goes to the Almighty Father, His steadfast love endures forever.

I acknowledged the contributions of various scholars / authors whose works provided the framework of the publication.

I am especially grateful to my parents, Chief Titus and Chief Mrs. Beatrice Nwosu (Umuikpa Ihite Azia, Ihiala Local Government Area of Anambra State, Nigeria), I also thank my siblings for their words of encouragement, all round supports to see to the success of this work.

I acknowledge also my congregation –Daughters of Mary Mother of Mercy, my Superior General and councilors, our Sisters Kate Nweke, Amabillis Onuoha and Calistus Nwaezeakpo in particular for their support and encouragement to me.

My gratitude also goes to my colleague Dr. M.J Abubakar, Ahmadu Bello University Zaria, my special father Prof J.B Babalola, Federal University of Ibadna (UI). I appreciate in particularly the encouragement from my Head of Department – Prof Emenika Obi, My erudite scholars/colleagues, lecturers, students in Department of Educational Management and Policy, my Dean of the Faculty- Prof Eze and our able vice Chancellors-both former and present –Prof Ahaneku and Prof Esimone, all in Nnamdi Azikiwe University, Awka, Nigeria.

The prayers and words of encouragement from my fathers in

faith Rt Rev Dr. H.O Okeke, Catholic Bishop of Nnewi Diocese, Most Rev Dr. V.M Okeke- Metropolitan of Onitsha Ecclesiastical province, Most Rev. Dr. L.I Ugorji – Catholic Bishop of Umuahia Diocese, are appreciated.

I acknowledged the prayers and encouragements of Very Rev. Fr. Bona Chritus Umeogu, Dean, Faculty of Arts, Nnamdi Azikiwe University Awka.

The prayers and encouragement of Umu-Nduru, my Flower girls, the spiritual Director, Very Rev Fr. Emmanuel Obimma (Ebube Muonso)-Holy Ghost Adoration Ministry, Uke, Anambra state, remain evergreen in my grateful memory. I appreciate also our able Governor His Excellency Chief Dr. Willie Obiano, some government parastatals, Chief Dr. Victor Oye.

I will not forget to acknowledge the positive/beautiful experiences I gathered from my colleagues in the former place of work especially from Economics Department, Department of Educational Foundations and Administration, Nwafor Orizu College of Education, Nsugbe, Anambra State.

Finally, my gratitude goes to my special friends and well wishers for your prayers, patience and supports to me.

God bless you all.

Rev. Sr. Dr. Nwosu
Ogochukwu Hororata
(Dmmm)
2020

PREFACE

Information and Communication Technologies (ICTs) have become one of the basic building blocks of the society. The integration of ICT into education (primary, secondary and tertiary) has developed in different ways and in different countries and regions at various times.

The role of technology in teaching and learning has become one of the most important and widely discussed issues in contemporary education engineering. Most experts in the field of education agree that when properly used, information and communication technology (ICT) hold great promise to improve teaching and learning in addition to shaping the workforce opportunities.

Additionally, in the rapid changing world of global market competition, automation and increasing democratization, higher education is necessary for an individual to have the capacity and capability to access and apply information.

This textbook on Information and Communication Technology and the Management of schools in Nigeria provides a comprehensive coverage on what educational planners and administrators, researchers, teachers, students and pupils need to know about ICT, for their usefulness and for effective teaching and learning in Nigeria.

This book which contains five major chapters is written

in easy-to-read and easy-to-understand style; written with conviction and logically arranged for clear exposition of ICT and management of various levels of schools in Nigeria.

I wish to express my sincere gratitude to my siblings and especially my brother, Dr. Martin Nwosu for their support and candid advice to me to publish this work, my mentor. Prof. J.B Babalolo, University of Ibadan, My colleague Dr M.J Abubakar, Ahmadu Bello University Zaria for his support and encouragement. My present Head of Department of Educational Management and Policy, Nnamdi Azikiwe University, Awka, Prof. Emenike Obi, and my dear lecturers/ colleagues erudite scholars in our department.

Rev. Sr. Dr. Nwosu Ogochukwu
Honorata (DMMM)
Department of Educational
Management and Policy.
Nnamdi Azikiwe University, Awka

CHAPTER ONE

CONCEPT OF INFORMATION COMMUNICATION TECHNOLOGY (ICT)

Introduction

This chapter attempts to introduce the reader to basic concept of ICT, the types, its importance, historical perspective in term of usage in Nigeria and the need for it application in schools in Nigeria. ICTs have become one of the basic building blocks of modern society. Many societies/countries now regard understanding the basic skills and concepts of ICT as part of the core of education, alongside reading, writing and numeracy. However, there appears to be a misconception that ICTs generally refers to 'computers and computing related activities'. This is fortunately not the case, although computers and their application play a significant role in modern information management, other technologies and/or systems also comprise of the phenomenon that is commonly regarded as ICTs

The integration of ICT into education has developed in different ways in different countries and regions, at different times – sometimes starting at the upper secondary level and spreading downwards through the lower secondary to primary to early childhood education; sometimes at the primary level spreading both upwards and downwards; sometimes through the establishment of Computer Science or Informatics or ICT as a school subject, which then broadens out to affect other subjects and other teachers (UNESCO, 2012).

Meaning of ICT

ICT stands for information & communication technologies. ICT refers to technologies that provide access to information through communications. It is similar to information technology (IT). "But primarily focuses on communication technologies. This includes the internet, wireless network, cell phones & other communications medium". In the past few decades information &communication technologies have provided to society with vastarray of a new communication capabilities. "People can communicate in real time with others in different countries using technologies such as instant messaging, voice over IP and video conferencing, social networking

Websites like face book allow users from all over the world to remain in contact and communicate on a regular basis". Modern information communication technologies have created a global village in which people communicate with others across the world as if they were living next door (Muhammad, Irfanullah & Siraj-u-Din, 2015)

Components of ICT

ICTs can be divided into two components:

1. Information and Communication Infrastructure (ICI): This refers to physical telecommunication systems and networks (cellular, broadcast, cable, satellite, postal) as well as the services that utilize them (Internet, voice, mail, radio, and television).
2. Information Technology (IT): This refers to the hardware and software, networks, and media for collection, storage, processing, transmission and presentation of information.
   (Katundu, 2000 &UNESCO, 2012).

Characteristics of ICT

1. Acquisition
2. Storage
3. Manipulation
4. Management
5. Transmission or reception of data or information.
6. Real time access to information.
7. Easy availability of updated data.
8. Connecting Geographically dispersed regions.
9. Wider range of communication media.

Concept of ICT as Viewed by Scholars

Information and Communication Technology refers to as a computer based facilities used by organization personnel to record, transmit, generate, retrieve, impact knowledge and process information and communication needs (Asiyai, 2010).

Mueen, Asadullah, Raed&Jamshed (2013) defined ICT to include electronic network-embodying complex hardware and software-linked by a vast array of technical protocol.

In the opinion of Ufuophu and Ayobami (2012) ICTs include internet, satellite, cable data transmission and computer assisted equipment.ICT in the view of Opara and Onyije (2014) are facilities, tools or resources that could be used to process, store, preserve, access, retrieve, and disseminate information with ease.

Adebayo (2013) defines Information and Communication Technology (ICT) as technologythat supports activities involving the creation, storage, manipulation and communication of information. ICTs could be viewed as a diverse set of technological tools and resources used to communicate and to create, disseminate, store and manage information.UNESCO (2002) viewed information and communication technology (ICT) as the combination of 'Informatics technology' with other related technology, specifically communication technology

Steve and Diepreye, (2009) defined ICT as an eclectic application of computing, communication, telecommunication and satellite technology. Benamati and Serva, (2007) ICT is a form of technology that is used to transmit, store, create, share or exchange information.

Laukkanen, (2007) views ICT as, a generic term referring to technologies which are used for collecting, storing editing and passing information in various forms.

ICT, are facilities, tools or resources that could be used to process, store, preserve, access, retrieve and disseminate information with ease. It could be seen as the engine for growth and tool for empowerment, with profound implications for education, change and socio-economic development (Ayoade, 2014).

From the following definitions of ICT advanced by some experts, summarily, ICT can be refers to as any technology that students and teachers use to organize, create, manipulate, solve, find, draw, design, synthesize, share, collaborate, modify, analyze, evaluate and disseminate information. ICT offer flexibility, engage and motivate learners and therefore encourage a learner centered approach to teaching.

Objectives of ICT in Education

The objectives of the federal government of Nigeria on Information Technology (NIT) as highlighted by Yusuf, (2005) are:

1. Making Information and Communication Technologies (ICT) mandatory at all levels of education
2. Developing ICTs curricula for primary, secondary and tertiary institutions
3. Provision of study grants and scholarship on ICT
4. Training the trainer scheme for National Youth Service Corps members ICT capacity development at zonal, state and local levels

Types of ICT Devices and Applications

ICT stands for information & communications technology is an umbrella term that includes any communication device, as well as the various services and applications associated with them encompassing;

1. Teleconferencing,
2. Email,
3. Audio Conferencing,
4. Television Lessons,
5. Radio Broadcasts,
6. Interactive Radio Counselling,
7. Interactive Voice Response System,
8. Audiocassettes, and
9. Network hardware and software
10. Satellite systems
11. Videoconferencing
12. Distance learning
13. CD ROMs (Sharma, 2003; Sanyal, 2001; Bhattacharya and Sharma, 2007;Abe &Adu, 2007)

Importance of ICT in Education

The field of education has been affected by ICTs, which have undoubtedly affected teaching, learning, and research. A great deal of research has proven the benefits to the quality of education. In the wards of Yusuf (2005),Plomp, Pelgrumand Law (2007), Lim and Chai(2004), Bhattacharya and Sharma, 2007; Cholin, (2005) ICTs have the potential to:

1. Innovate, accelerate, enrich and deepen skills
2. Motivate and engage students
3. Help relate school experience to work practices
4. Create economic viability for tomorrow's workers
5. As well as strengthening teaching and helping schools change
6. Help people keep pace with the latest developments

7. Remove communication barriers such as that of space and time

8. Allow for the creation of digital resources like digital libraries

9. Empower teachers and learners, transforming teaching and learning processes from being highly teacher-dominated to student-centered.

10. Allow learners to develop their creativity, problem-solving abilities, informational reasoning skills, communication skills, and other higher-order thinking skills

Historical Perspective of use of ICT use in Nigeria

Near the end of 1980s, the term 'computers' was replaced by IT' (information technology), signifying a shift of focus from computing technology to the capacity to store and retrieve information. This was followed by the introduction of the term 'ICT' (information and communication technology) around 1992, when e-mail started to become available to the general public Pelgrum and Law (2003). According to a United Nations report (1999), ICTs cover Internet service provision, telecommunications equipment and services, information technology equipment and services, media and broadcasting, libraries and documentation centers, commercial information providers, network-based information services, Two and other related information and communication activities.

The 1990s was the decade of computer communications and information access, particularly with the popularity and accessibility of internet-based services such as electronic mail and the World Wide Web (WWW). At the same time the CD-ROM became the standard for distributing packaged software (replacing the floppy disk). As a result, educators became more focused on the use of the technology to improve student learning as a rationale for investment. Any discussion about the use of computer systems in schools is built upon an understanding of the link between schools, learning and computer technology. When the potential use of computers in schools was first mooted, the predominant conception was that students would be 'taught' by computers (Mevarech& Light, 1992)

It would be recalled that The Federal Ministry of Education launched an ICT-driven project know as School Net(www. snng.org) (Federal Republic of Nigeria, (2006); Adomi(2005); Okebukola(2004), which was intended to equip all schools in Nigeria with computers and communications technologies. In June 2003, at the African Summit of the World Economic Forum held in Durban, South Africa, the New Partnership for African Development (NEPAD) launched the e-Schools Initiative, intended to equip all African high schools with ICT equipment including computers, radio and television sets, phones and fax machines, communication equipment, scanners, digital cameras, and copiers, among other things. It is also meantto connect African students to the Internet. The NEPAD capacity-building initiative was to be executed over aten-year period, with the high school component being completed in the first five years. Three phases are envisaged, with fifteen to twenty countries in each phase. The phases are to be staggered, and an estimated 600,100 schools are expected to benefit. The aim of the initiative is to impart ICT skills to young Africans in primary and secondary schools, and to harness ICT to improve, enrich, and expand education in African countries Aginam(2006).

Although efforts have been made to ensure that ICTs are available and used in Nigerian secondary schools, the level of uptake has remarkably improved in recent years.

Need for ICT Application in Nigeria schools

The demand for computer/ICT literacy is increasing in Nigeria, because employees realize that

Computers and other ICT facilities can enhance efficiency. On the other hand, employees have also realized that computers can be a threat to their jobs, and the only way to enhance job security is to become computer literate. With the high demand for computer literacy, the teaching and learning of these skills has become a concern among professionals Oduroye (2012). This is also true of other ICT components.

In a rapidly changing world, basic education is essential for an individual be able to access and apply information. Such ability must find include ICTs in the global village. Conventional teaching has emphasized content. For many years course have been written around textbooks. Teachers have taught through lectures and presentations interspersed with tutorials and learning activities designed to consolidate and rehearse the content. Contemporary settings are now favouring curricula that promote competency and performance. Curricula are starting to emphasize capabilities and to be concerned more with how the information will be used than with what the information is. Contemporary ICTs are able to provide strong support for all these requirements and there are now many outstanding examples of world class settings for competency and performance-based curricula that make sound use of the affordances of these technologies (Oliver, 2000)

ICT application and use will prove beneficial in improving Nigeria's educational system and giving students a better education. A technologically-advanced workforce will lead to ICT growth in Nigeria, with the potential to improve military technology and telecommunications, media communications, and skilled ICT professionals who will be well-equipped to solve IT problems in Nigeria and other parts of the world (Goshit, 2006).

CHAPTER TWO

ICT IN EDUCATION MANAGEMENT

Introduction

ICT and school management is an important issue, since it is well recognized that senior managers in schools have a major impact upon classroom and curriculum practices, and the use of ICT within schools is permeating aspects of school practice to the extent that it will impact upon the practice of all staff (both teaching and non-teaching). By implication, the field of ICT and school management is a vital field to explore, to support appropriately both current and future practice.

ICT refers to a collection of computer-based technologies, which are exploited to support teaching and learning, communication and collaboration, self-expression, creation, etc., that is, for the promotion of all developmental domains of children, and learners of any age. In past, it was considered that the computer would 'take over' the teacher's job in the same way as a robot computer may take over a welder's job. It therefore became rather imaginative where "a small child sits alone with a computer". However, the use of information and communication technologies in the educative process has been divided into two broad categories: ICTs for Education and ICTs in Education

1. **ICT for Education:** ICTs for education refers to the development of information and communications technology specifically for teaching/learning purposes.
2. **ICT in Education:** ICTs in education involves the adoption of general components of information and communication technologies in the teaching learning process.

ICT for Education is used in the following ways:

1. To broadcast material, online facility or CD-ROM can be used as sources of information in different subjects
2. To facilitate communication for pupils with special needs
3. To use electronic toys to develop spatial awareness and psycho-motor control
4. To use the Online resource like, email, Chat, discussion forum to support collaborative writing and sharing of information
5. To facilitate video-conferencing or other form of Tele conferencing to involve wide range of students from distant Geographic areas
6. For Blended learning by combining conventional classroom learning with E-leaming learning systems
7. To process administrative and assessment data
8. To exchange and share ideas -among teachers for the professional growth
9. To carry out internet-based research to enhance, educational process

ICT in Education is used in the following ways:

1. To positively impact on teaching, learning, and research.
2. To affect the delivery of education and enable wider access to the same.
3. To increase flexibility so that learners can access the education regardless of time and geographical barriers.
4. To influence the way students are taught and how they learn.
5. To provide rich environment and motivation for teaching learning process.
6. To have a profound impact on the process of learning in education by offering new possibilities for learners and teachers.
7. These possibilities can have an impact on student performance and achievement.
8. To provide wider availability of best practices and best course material in education.
9. To foster better teaching and improved academic achievement of students.

ICTs Available and Relevant to Education

In recent years there has been a groundswell of interest in how computers and the Internet can best be harnessed to improve the efficiency and effectiveness of education at all levels and in both formal and non-formal settings. "But ICTs are more than just these technologies; older technologies such as the telephone, radio and television, although now given less attention, have a longer and richer history as instructional tools". For instance, radio and television have for over forty years been used for open and distance learning, although print remains the cheapest, most accessible and therefore most dominant delivery mechanism in both developed and developing countries(Aribamikan, 2007).

The Following are Some ICTs Available and Relevant to Education

1. **e-learning:** Although most commonly associated with higher education and corporate training, e-learning encompasses learning at all levels, both formal and non-formal, that uses an information network—the Internet, an intranet (LAN) or extranet (WAN)—whether wholly or in part, for course delivery, interaction, evaluation and/ or facilitation. "Others prefer the term online learning. Web-based learning is a subset of e-learning and refers to learning using an Internet mainly using a browser (such as Chrome or Firefox or Internet Explorer)". It can alsobe viewed as learning through the use of electronic devices.

2. **Blended Learning:** Another term that is gaining currency is blended learning. "This refers to learning models that combine traditional classroom practice with e-learning solutions". For example, students in a traditional class can be assigned both print-based and online materials, have online mentoring sessions with their teacher through chat, and are subscribed to a class email list. "Or a Web-based training course can be enhanced by periodic face-to face instruction". Blending was prompted by the recognition that not all learning is best achieved in an electronically-mediated environment, particularly one that dispenses with a live instructor altogether. Instead, consideration must be given to the subject matter, the learning objectives and outcomes, the characteristics of the learners, and the learning context in order to arrive at

the optimum mix of instructional and delivery methods (Asiabeka, 2010)

3. **Open and distance learning:** Open and distance learning is defined by the Commonwealth of Learning as a way of providing learning opportunities that is characterized by the separation of teacher and learner in time or place, or both time and place; learning that is certified in some way by an institution or agency; the use of a variety of media, including print and electronic; two-way communications that allow learners and tutors to interact; the possibility of occasional face-to-face meetings; and a specialized division of labor in the production and delivery of courses. Using the various technologies available for video conferencing, educators can provide a more interactive distance learning experience by delivering real-time, bidirectional video, voice, and data communications to their distance students, rather than just the standard electronic media.

4. **Videoconferencing:** Videoconferencing is a method of communicating between two or more locations in which sound, vision and data signals are conveyed electronically to enable simultaneous interactive communication. Much more personal and effective than audio conferencing, all parties involved can see the facial expressions and body language that are so vital to the way we communicate JNT Association (2007). Modern standalone video conferencing units provide advanced video and audio quality due to more efficient compression and can function over normal broadband internet connections. Video conference participants use either VC system, web based application or on premise software to interactively communicate with co-workers, students and others in

virtual meetings or classrooms. This approach is easier, cheaper and much more convenient to use while also providing easy access to file sharing and variety of others collaborative services. Roberts, (2009).

Components of Video Conference

Videoconferencing has three essential components:

The Hardware. The hardware components include a camera, microphone, a video conferencing unit, display unit, and audio system

1. **The intervening network that carries the signals between sites**. This consist of internet protocol (IP) networks and integrated system digital network (ISDN). With IP transmission, the results can be variable as the videoconference data has to compete with other computing data. ISDN guarantees connections at the selected quality, giving more reliable conferences

2. **The conference environment or room**. Lighting is an easy way to improve picture quality. If the room is not specially built or equipped for video conferencing, it is probable that there are not enough lights to provide the optimum quality for the video conference cameras. The result is a flickering visual noise seen especially when the cameras are zoomed in Sami (2008). Another result is a lack of colour saturation. Thus proper lightning is an easy way to improve video quality. Also, the room should be well acoustically designed to avoid the echo.

Benefits of Video Conferencing

1. Sharing of presentations
2. It allows immediate, full two way communication of content; verbal, pictorial objects etc.
3. Greater access to experts/specialists (nationally and internationally)
4. More productive use of time (eliminates wasted travel time) and significant travel cost savings.
5. Reduced environmental impact through less travel and reduced pressure, stress and fatigue from travel.
6. Facilitating short notice meetings between individuals in distant locations thus decisions can be made more quickly.
7. Increased meeting attendance by participants who would otherwise be unable to join in
8. Greater accessibility and allows geographical reach even to rural or remote locations.
9. A conference session can be saved for future reference e.g. class notes can be saved and distributed via network for references by students (Alan, 2009).

Disadvantages of Video Conferencing

1. It may lead to laziness with some students as they can have their classes while at home thus lacking self discipline.
2. Lack of interpersonal relationship between students and teachers or between students themselves.
3. The technology may degrade the received images and sound. Body language can be lost if image movement is jerky. There can be a delay on the sound too.
4. The atmosphere of a face-to-face meeting is lost.

5. For meetings, videoconferences are more effective if the participants already know each other.

6. The security may be compromised as one can hack onto a private VC session (Alan, 2009).

Interactive Radio Counselling

There is, however, a low-cost educational technology with a long history that has demonstrated positive impact in many developing countries -- educational radio, specially what is known as interactive radio instruction (IRI). Interactive radio instruction (IRI) is a distance education system that combines radio broadcasts with active learning to improve educational quality and teaching practices. IRI has been in use for more than 25 years and has demonstrated that it can be effective on a large scale at low cost. IRI programs require teachers and students to react verbally and physically to questions and exercises posed by radio characters and to participate in group work, experiments, and other activities suggested by the radio program.

Importance of ICT to Students

The use of ICT in educational settings, by itself acts as a catalyst for change in this domain. ICTs by their very nature are tools that encourage and support independent learning. Students using ICTs for learning purposes become immersed in the process of learning and as more and more students use computers as information sources and cognitive tools Reeves andJonassen(1996), the influence of the technology on supporting how students learn will continue to increase.

The Following are Specific Importance of ICT to Students;

1. ICT increases the flexibility of delivery of education
2. Increase learners access knowledge anytime and from anywhere.
3. It influence the way students are taught and how they learn
4. It makes teaching and learning processes learner driven and not by teachers.
5. it better prepare the learners for lifelong learning as well as to improve the quality of learning.
6. it also removes many of the temporal constraints that face learners with special needs .
7. With the help of ICT, students can now browse through e-books, sample examination papers, previous year papers etc.
8. ICT also allows the academic institutions to reach disadvantaged groups and new international educational markets
9. Learners can also have easy access to resource persons, mentors, experts, researchers, professionals, and peers- all over the world.(Moore and Kearsley, 1996)

Maintenance of ICT Facilities for Effective Educational Management

Maintenance is the combination of all technical and administrative functions, intended to retain an item in, or restore it to a state in which it can perform its required function. It includes routine, preventive, predictive, emergency and corrective maintenance employed in putting the facility back to a state in which they will continue to perform their intended function as originally conceived (Olatunji, Aghimien and Ayodeji, 2016).

Maintenance of ICT facilities becomes inevitable in order to ensure it continuous use and accomplish desire objective in educational management. Specifically, the following are ways of maintaining ICT for educational management;

1. **Planned Maintenance**: The maintenance organized and carried out with fore thought, control and the use of records to a predetermined plan

2. **Unplanned Maintenance**: The maintenance carried out to no predetermined plan. This is the restoration of sudden defective facility to its functional state

3. **Preventive Maintenance**: The maintenance carried out at predetermined intervals or corresponding to research criteria and intended to reduce the probability of failure or the performance degradation of an item.

4. **Corrective Maintenance**: The maintenance carried out after a failure has occurred and intended to restore an item to a state in which it can perform its required function. This maintenance strategy is simple and straightforward, "fix it when it breaks" (Mobley, 2004)

5. **Emergency Maintenance**: The maintenance which is carried out as a result of damage or breakdown of a structure, machine or system. It requires immediate or prompt action

6. **Condition-based Maintenance:** The preventive maintenance initiated as a result of knowledge of the condition of an item from routine or continuous monitoring

7. **Schedule Maintenance:** Is a type of maintenance practice carried out at specific interval in accordance with guideline of inform of manual or experts advice

Conditions for the use of ICT in the Class by the Teacher

The integration of information and communication technologies can help revitalize teachers and students. This can help to improve and develop the quality of education by providing curricular support in difficult subject areas. To achieve these objectives, teachers need to be involved in collaborative projects and development of intervention change strategies, which would include teaching partnerships with ICT as a tool.

The followings are Conditions for Teachers Use of ICT in the Classrooms:

1. Teachers must believe in the effectiveness of technology
2. Teachers must believe that the use of technology will not cause any disturbances
3. Teachers must believe that they have control over technology (Zhao &Cziko 2001)

ICT for Enhanced Quality and Accessibility of Education

Information and communication technology has been so embraced that it is used severally in many ways to improve the quality and accessibility to education anywhere and anytime. Scholars such as (Bhattacharya and Sharma, 2007; Cholin, 2005;Sanyal, 2001; Mooij, 2007; Cross and Adam, 2007; UNESCO, 2002; Chandra and Patkar, 2007; Bottino, 2003; Mason, 2000; Lim and Hang, 2003and Yuen, 2003)have been able to identify ways through which ICT has enhanced the quality of education, among which are;

1. ICT allows for the creation of digital resources like digital libraries where the students, teachers and professionals

can access research material and course material from any place at any time.

2. ICT facilities allow the networking of academics and researchers and hence sharing of scholarly material. This avoids duplication of work

3. ICT eliminates time barriers in education for learners as well as teacher. It eliminates geographical barriers as learners can log on from any place.

4. ICT provides new educational approaches. It can provide speedy dissemination of education to target disadvantaged groups

5. ICT enhances the international dimension of educational services. It can also be used for non-formal education like health campaigns and literacy campaigns.

6. Use of ICT in education develops higher order skills such as collaborating across time and place and solving complex real world problems

7. It improves the perception and understanding of the world of the student.

8. ICT can be used to prepare the workforce for the information society and the new global economy

9. Use of ICT is motivating for the students as well as for the teachers themselves.

10. It also improves the quality of education by facilitating learning by doing, real time conversation, delayed time conversation, directed instruction, self-learning, problem solving, information seeking and analysis, and critical thinking, as well as the ability to communicate, collaborate and learn.

ICT for Enhanced Learning Environment

ICT presents an entirely new learning environment for students, thus requiring a different skill set to be successful. ICT is changing processes of teaching and learning by adding elements of vitality to learning environments including virtual environments for the purpose. ICT is a potentially powerful tool for offering educational opportunities. It is difficult and maybe even impossible to imagine future learning environments that are not supported, in one way or another, by Information and Communication Technologies (ICT).

When looking at the current widespread diffusion and use of ICT in modern societies, especially by the young the so-called digital generation then it should be clear that ICT will affect the complete learning process today and in the future Collins (1996). Learning environments need to reflect the potential uses of knowledge that pupils are expected to master, in order to prevent the acquired knowledge from becoming inert (Bransford, Sherwood, Hasselbring, Kinzer, & Williams, 1990; Duffy & Knuth, 1990).

In addition, teachers should stimulate pupils to engage in active knowledge construction. This calls for open-ended learning environments instead of learning environments which focus on a mere transmission of facts Collins (1996); Hannafin, Hall, Land and Hill, (1994); Jonassen, Peck, & Wilson, (1999). ICT may contribute to creating powerful learning environments in numerous ways:

1. Viewing information from multiple perspectives
2. Fostering the authenticity of learning environments

3. Making complex processes easier to understand through simulations that contribute to authentic learning environments
4. Facilitating active learning and higher-order thinking
5. Fostering co-operative learning and reflection about the content
6. Serve as a tool to curriculum differentiation
7. Providing opportunities for adapting the learning content and tasks to the needs and capabilities of each individual pupil and by providing tailored feedback (Alexander, 1999; Jonassen, 1999; Susman, 1998; Mooij, 1999; Smeets&Mooij, 2001).

Kennewell (2000) feel it is essential that computers be placed in the classroom, in order to maximize the opportunities for curriculum activity. ICT environment improves the experience of the students and teachers and to use intensively the learning time for better results. The ICT environment has been developed by using different software and also the extended experience in developing web based and multimedia materials. ICTs have an important role to play in changing and modernizing educational systems and ways of learning.

ICT for Enhanced Learning Motivation

With ICT, what could probably be written on a piece of paper, if it is done on the computer it is more entertaining, interesting, giving the students a different taste of action. Even where ICT is not used to change the pedagogy, it can have an impact on the motivation of learners. Students can generate their own knowledge, in other words, they can build concepts which have not been previously given. This new method promotes reflection, critical judgment, it makes students improve their own operational abilities, it makes them carry out a thorough analysis of what they are studying.

ICTs can enhance the quality of education in several ways,

1. by increasing learner motivation and engagement,
2. by facilitating the acquisition of basic skills,
3. by enhancing teacher training.
4. by promoting the shift to a learner centered environment.
5. ICTs, especially computers and Internet technologies, enable new ways of teaching and learning rather than simply allow teachers and students to do what they have done before in a better way.
6. ICT has an impact not only on what students learn, but it also plays a major role on how the students learn.
7. Along with a shift of curricula from "content-centered" to "competence-based", the mode of curricula delivery has now shifted from "teacher centered" forms of delivery to "student-centered" forms of delivery. ICT provides-Motivation to Learn.

ICTs such as videos, television and multimedia, computer software that combine text, sound, and colourful moving images can be used to provide challenging and authentic content that will engage the student in the learning process. Interactive radio likewise makes use of sound effects, songs, dramatizations, comic skits, and other performance conventions to compel the students to listen and become more involved in the lessons being delivered. It is convincing that children feel more motivated than before in such type of teaching in the classroom rather than the stereotype 45 minutes lecture. This type of learning process is much more effective than the monotonous monologue classroom situation where the teacher just lectures from a raised platform and the students just listen to the teacher.

ICT changes the characteristics of problems and learning tasks, and hence play an important task as mediator of cognitive development, enhancing the acquisition of generic cognitive competencies as essential for life in our knowledge society. Students using ICTs for learning purposes become immersed in the process of learning and as more and more students use computers as information sources and cognitive tools, the influence of the technology on supporting how students learn will continue to increase. Learning approaches using contemporary ICTs provide many opportunities for constructivist learning through their provision and support for resource-based, student centered settings and by enabling learning to be related to context and to practice (Reeves and Jonassen, 1996 ; Berge, 1998; Barron, 1998).

The teachers could make their lessons more attractive and lively by using multi-media and on the other hand the students will be able to capture the lessons taught to them easily. As they found the class very interesting, the teaching is also retained in their minds for a longer span which support them during the time of examination. More so than any other type of ICT, networked computers with Internet connectivity can increase learner motivation as it combines the media richness and interactivity of other ICTs with the opportunity to connect with real people and to participate in real world events. ICT-enhanced learning is student-directed and diagnostic. Unlike static, text- or print-based educational technologies, ICT-enhanced learning recognizes that there are many different learning pathways and many different articulations of knowledge. ICTs allow learners to explore and discover rather than merely listen and remember. The World Wide Web (WWW) also provides a virtual international gallery for students' work. ICT can engage and inspire students, and this has been cited as a factor influencing ready adaptors of ICT (Long, 2001; Loveless, 2003&Wood, 2004).

ICT for Enhanced Scholastic Performance

Based on the extensive usage of ICTs in education the need appeared to unravel the myth that surrounds the use of information and communication technology (ICT) as an aid to teaching and learning, and the impact it has on students' academic performance. ICTs are said to help expand access to education, strengthen the relevance of education to the increasingly digital workplace, and raise educational quality. However, the experience of introducing different ICTs in the classroom and other educational settings all over the world over the past several decades suggests that the full realization of the potential educational benefits of ICT. The direct link between ICT use and students' academic performance has been the focus of extensive literature during the last two decades. ICT helps students in their learning process by improving the communication between them and the instructors (Valasidou&Bousiou, 2005).

The analysis of the effects of the methodological and technological innovations on the students' attitude towards the learning process and on students' performance seems to be evolving towards a consensus, according to which an appropriate use of digital technologies in education can have significant positive effects both on students' attitude and their achievement. Research has shown that the appropriate use of ICTs can catalyze the paradigmatic shift in both content and pedagogy that is at the heart of education reform in the 21st century. Kulik's (1994) opined that meta-analysis study revealed that, on average, students who used ICT-based instruction scored higher than students without computers. The students also learned more in less time and liked their classes more when ICT-based instruction was included. In a related development, Fuchs and Woessman (2004) used international data from the Programme for International Student Assessment (PISA),and discovered that while the bivariate correlation between the availability of ICT and students' performance is strongly and significantly positive, the correlation becomes small and insignificant when other student environment characteristics are taken into consideration.

There exist the relationship between having a home computer and school performance, as suggested by Attwell and Battle (1999) that students who have access to a computer at home for educational purposes, have improved scores in reading and math. It was further discovered by Becker (2000) that ICT increases student engagement, which leads to an increased amount of time students spend working outside class.. ICTs especially computers and Internet technologies enable new ways of teaching and learning rather than simply allow teachers and students to do what they have done before in a better way. ICT helps in providing a catalyst for rethinking teaching practice, developing the kind of graduates and citizens required in an information society ; improving educational outcomes and enhancing and improving the quality of teaching and learning (Wagner, 2001; McCormick & Scrimshaw, 2001;Flecknoe,2002; Garrison & Anderson, 2003).

ICT can help deepen students' content knowledge, engage them in constructing their own knowledge, and support the development of complex thinking skills Kozma,(2005) ; Kulik, (2003); Webb and Cox (2004).Studies have identified a variety of constructivist learning strategies (e.g., students work in collaborative groups or students create products that represent what they are learning) that can change the way students interact with the content. The use of asynchronous CMC tools to promote student self-efficacy and academic performance was suggested by Albert Bandura, Girasoli and Hannafin (2008). ICTs have the potential for increasing access to and improving the relevance and quality of education. The use of ICT in educational settings, by itself acts as a catalyst for change in this domain. Students using ICTs for learning purposes become immersed in the process of learning and as more and more students use computers as information sources and cognitive tools), the influence of the technology on supporting how students learning will continue to increase.

ICT as Tool for Educational Management

The prevailing condition in school management in Nigeria is disheartening and discouraging. The country seems to be living in prehistoric times in the educational management while even developing countries in Africa such as South Africa, Kenya, Uganda and Tanzania are far ahead of Nigeria in ICT applications. Despite its huge material resources and population endowment, Nigeria cannot be counted among progressive nations using ICT in educational management, as technology has become a critical tool for achieving success in education. Samuel and Ede (2005)

There are lots of ICT application tools that have been widely used in school management. Available ICT applications for educational administrative purposes include internet, websites, software and hardware such as printers, photocopy machines, scanner and computer (Kazi, 2012; Mwalong, 2011 &Susmita, 2007).

ICT Tools widely used in School Management are:

1. **Internet- Based Tools**: In the last two to three decades, the internet and ICT application tools have been expanded into the field of education all over the world. This is due to capabilities of internet to provide opportunities for introducing advanced teaching-learning methods. The advanced modern methods of teaching and learning helped in preparing students for future workforce. Internet based searching, communication and managing materials which will directly or indirectly increase the school performance (Gharifekr, 2012).

2. **Hardware Application**: As year passes by, computers and other information, communication and technology evolved. New machines, new equipment created and new opportunities especially in school administration, which make the management process easier, faster and cheaper. We can see that ICT application tools have equipped school management such as computer work, photocopy machines, TV, radio, digital camera, scanner, DVD players, laptops, multimedia projectors and overhead projectors (Mwalongo, 2011; Richardson, 2007)

3. **Software Applications**: A School manager tends to use various software applications for their job management purposes. The most frequently used applications in the management of schools are: Microsoft word, Excel and power point, spread sheet and database.

CHAPTER THREE

ICT AND THE MANAGEMENT OF PRIMARY SCHOOLS

Introduction

In most Nigeria schools, officials still go through the laborious exercise of manually registering students, maintaining records of pupil, performance, keeping inventory list of supplies, doing cost accounting, paying bills, printing reports and drawing architectural designs. The huge man-hour spend on these exercises can be drastically reduced with ICT to enhance overall management procedure. Computers bring great speed and accuracy to each of these aforementioned tasks, along with the convenience of storing large quantities of information on small disks or tapes. Nigeria cannot afford to lag behind in using multimedia to raise the intellectual and creative resources of her citizens. This is particularly important for children whose adulthood will blossom in a cyber environment entirely different from that of the present Nigerian children need to be taught by radically new educational programme and variety of There are many benefits to using ICT to teach literacy. ICT allows the teacher to produce and modify resources quickly and easily. It allows access to a wide range of information in various formats, and interactive whiteboards (IWBs) have become essential tools in the classroom.

Importance of ICT in Primary Schools

1. To provide technology for better instruction
2. To provide tools for creative self-expression
3. To support children's learning and thinking processes
4. To provide special educational needs
5. To provide educational robotics and programming for children (UNESCO, 2012).

Classification of ICT as used in the Classroom

ICT may serve various roles in schools for the purpose of enhancing students 'learning. Based on how an ICT tool is used in the classroom, Lim and Tay (2003) classified ICT tools into four types:

1. **Information Tools:** These are applications that provide information in various formats (e.g., text, sound, graphics or video). Examples include multimedia encyclopedias or resources available in the World-Wide Web(www).
2. **Situating Tools:** These are systems that situate students in an environment where they may "experience" a context and happenings. Such systems include simulations, games and virtual reality.
3. **Construction Tools:** These are usually tools that can be used for manipulating information, organizing one's

ideas or representing one's interpretations. For instance, mind mapping or social networking applications that allow students to organize their ideas or reflections, and communicate these ideas and share with others.

4. **Communication Tools:** These are applications that facilitate communication between teacher and students or among students beyond the physical barrier (of space, time or both) of the classroom. The important examples are e-mail, e-conferencing and e-discussion boards.

5. **Tutorial Tools:** ICT tutorial tools allow students to navigate to different areas of a package depending on their personal interests or needs. It is designed to enhance students' reading and spelling through phonological awareness. The software is particularly useful for students having special needs. Research has shown that students with reading problems learn to decode words more effectively when given speech feedback through the use of tutorial tools

ICT and Primary School Supervision

Information and Communication Technology (ICT) is important in primary education because it enables kids to search for the information they need and to organize what they have found. As children progress through the school system, they become increasingly responsible for their own learning.

Modern supervision consists of positive, dynamic, democratic actions designed to improve instruction through the continued growth of all concerned individuals, the child, teacher, supervisor, administrator, and parents or other lay person. In this virtualized world and digital schools, supervision needs to improve and integrate a digital model of supervision.

Supervision has gone through many metamorphoses; supervisory behaviors and practices are affected by political, social, religious, and industrial forces in any country around the world (PasaMemisoglu,2007)

It is a common knowledge that instructional supervisors main responsibility is to help teachers build on their strengths, improve, and remain in the profession, instead of probing teachers' efficiencies and seeking their dismissal. Therefore, school supervision is generally seen as leadership that encourages a continuous involvement of all school personnel in a cooperative attempt to achieve the most effective school program.

Primary school supervision using ICT implies new forms of supervision to ensure proper alignment of teaching-learning methodologies, resources, and evaluation on digital learning environments and to understand how to implement right supervisory processes in contexts highly digitized. It should be borne in mind that supervision does not mean an inquisition or fault finding, but rather signifies guidance, assistance, and sharing of ideas with all those involved in the process of teaching and learning(Clark, 2001;Rutherford, 2004; Zapeda,2003&Sevillano, 2009).

ICT can be a valuable resource that serves to enhance both these functions and processes of supervision of school contexts mediated by ICT. Even where classrooms are well equipped with ICT, Rutherford (2004) observed that it is unlikely that most teachers will be able to exploit

the power of these tools without encouragement and support; hence, the first step towards the effective use of technology in classrooms should be fostering positive attitudes in teachers towards technology. This trend towards virtualized education needs new ways to monitor, control, counsel, and guide the entire school community for an effective and appropriate development of interactive models and virtual training. To fulfill these expectations, supervisors need considerable knowledge and skills to motivate and guide the teachers in their uses of ICT. This not only requires them to be computer literate, but also capable of helping teachers use computers and the Internet in teaching and learning as well as course design (Akbaba-Altun,2006)

As more teachers and students participate in online learning, inspectors will need to observe,

guide, and evaluate instruction in this digital environment that has altered the face-to-face classroom observation and evaluation model of instructional supervision. The virtual supervision needs to have direct access to digital activities of teachers and students on Learning Management Systems, and use in a proper way the tools in the supervisory functions; i.e. through the utilization of Internet Protocol -or IP-based videoconferencing equipment. However, IP is the preferred video format for this type of project due to its flexibility and cost. With IP video, there is no need for proprietary video lines, costly equipment or a high degree of technical skill (Collins, 2004& Anderson, 2004).

Advantages of Supervisory Application of ICT:

1. The technology enables the observation to occur as scheduled and archives it for subsequent review by the supervisor at another time.
2. A valid assessment of teacher and student performances is often compromised by the presence of an observer in the classroom; the technology certainly offers an interesting option to address this issue.
3. Finally, the teacher can view the archived observation prior to or during a post-observation conference. The

ability to zoom in on a particular teaching episode will enrich the conversation about best instructional practice as it relates to improved student performance (Esteban & Luisa, 2013)

ICT and Record Keeping in Primary Schools

On regular basis, information on school personnel (pupils, teachers and non-teachers),facilities, funds and school activities, are collected and preserved. This collection becomes school records. School records are therefore information or data which are collected on various aspects of a school and preserved for future use. Records are the documents that schools produce, keep and submit to parents, pupils, Educational Authorities and other stakeholders because, formal organizations like schools must account for whatever they do to justify their existence. School records therefore serve the following purposes:

1. Provide accurate and proper records of the students' achievement and growth from the point of entry to graduation
2. Ensure an up-to-date information on any school matter or students is made available on request
3. Facilitate collection of data or information which may be required for the purpose of planning, financing and reform for the educational and other sectors of the economy.
4. Provide information for guidance counselors and Inspectors
5. Provide referral information to employers of labour and other security agencies.

6. School records serve as a bank in which information is deposited and kept with the hope of retrieving for utilization.
7. Through records, especially the log-book, the history of the school could be known. Important events of the school are recorded in the log-book
8. School records also enables one know the termly and yearly academic performance of Students
9. School managers will be able to determine the academic progress of the students and take necessary precautionary measures towards improving their academic performance.
10. The financial status of the school could be determined through school records.
11. Income and expenditure of the school are entered into appropriate ledger, and this enhances accountability on the part of the school administrator.
12. School records also provide a basis for advisory and counselling services.
13. Teachers, head teachers and school counselors could make use of records in order to give advice on students' academic activities.
14. School records provide raw data which can be used by officials of education ministries for planning purposes

Trends in the development of ICT has revolutionalized the manner and volume of recordkeeping which enable us store substantial amount of data which can be easily retrieved, shared and copied. The ICT has provided us a wonderful opportunity to keep large volume of data at a little or less cost.

ICT became indispensable in the administration of schools. The principal through his secretarial staff deals with so many books and files containing information on what goes on in the school, who is in the school and what type of properties are owned by the school. Lawal (2001) stated clearly that it is no longer fashionable for a secretarial staff to write all the letters and prepare all other documents by hand or by the use of typewriter. Essentially, the following are the ICT facilities which are commonly used in an ideal office;

1. Computer
2. Printer
3. Internet services
4. Photocopying machine
5. Satellite disc
6. Diskettes
7. Flash drives
8. Laptops
9. Other electronic devices

ICT and Record Management in Schools

ICT assists the school principal to meet the task of school management in the area of record keeping. In view of the human factor involved, information or data which are written manually would often invariably results in errors, arrears of work thus giving room to misleading variables of decision-making as well as making information retrieval difficult

With the use of ICT, speed, accuracy, quick information retrieval and decision making can take place.ICT in schools enhances the daily school routine; input and output facilities which facilitates interrogation offices, alterations, displays and retrieval of information which are not possible with manual system can be done

Similarly, another important aspect of ICT facility is that data, information or records can be downloaded by the user without going through the pains of referring to source. For example there is no need for mails asking for the data, permission to release the data and replying or mailing the information requested by the individuals, organizations or parents.

The ICT facilities in the schools can be used to record, store information and facilitate learning by giving to students, staff and the general public access to the wonderful and unlimited information that the ICT provides.

ICT facilities save labour and also reduce the time spent on a job. They promote accuracy and prompt delivery of services, for instance the school's rules and regulations could be produced and given out to students on admission.

Principals are required to keep records through the use ICT not only because it is a statutory duty but because of its value in improving management practices.

The use of ICT in keeping school records provides accurate, timely, sufficient and relevant information, which are kept in the form of records and they provide information on the past, present and anticipated future activities of the school.

Types of Records in Primary Schools

The following records must be kept in every school by law and must be produced on request by any supervisor, Inspector and Ministry of Education officials:

1. Admission Register
2. Log Book
3. National Policy on Education
4. Attendance Register

5. School time-table
6. Diary of work (weekly)
7. Visitors book
8. Examination record book (C. A. Booklet)
9. Time/movement Register
10. Syllabus

Non-statutory records include among others the following:

1. Staff files
2. Lesson notes
3. Individual pupil's files
4. Discipline enforcement book
5. Examination result record (JSS/WAEC/NECO, ETC)
6. Advisory Board meeting
7. Parents Teachers Association (PTA)
8. Correspondence file
9. Finance file
10. Receipts
11. Cash Book
12. Public service rules
13. Financial Instruction
14. Stores regulations
15. Store Receive Voucher (SRV)
16. Store Issue Voucher (SIV)
17. Annual Performance Evaluation Reports (APER)
18. Health Records/Facilities
19. Hostel issues/Reports (Mani, 2013)

ICT and records management have a strong degree of commonality and many complementary expertise because they both concerns with creation, storage, accessibility and security of information. However, while ICT assists in engineering and maintaining systems to manage an institution's information assets, the focus of records management is protecting, classifying and maintaining the authenticity of records so that they remain accessible and function as evidence for as long as they are required to be (Visscher, Wild, &Fung, 2001)

Nakpodia (2011) asserts that the ultimate aim of records management and ICT in education institution is to support, protect and enable the institutions to manage students' records in a cost-effective manner now and in the future. ICT can draw on the expertise of the records managers to ensure the right information is being captured and records are classified in a way that promote their retrieval while protecting their sensitivities and are only kept to meet legal institution requirements and community expectations (Visscher,2001).

Challenges of using ICT in Record Keeping in Primary Schools

Application and services of Information and Communication Technology (ICT) are integral to any meaningful development in the education sector in all respects including record keeping. Thus the efficiency of employing ICT systems in record keeping may be seemingly difficult if the basic challenges of ICT are not addressed

Emetaron and Ibadin (2001),Osundina and otakhor (2007), and Ogunlade, (2008) identified the following as challenges to the use of ICT in primary schools:

1. **Lack of Basic and Adequate Infrastructures/Resources:** The non-existence of basic and adequate physical facilities such as accommodation space for computers with internet connectivity, electric generators and

adequate furniture pose great problems in the usage of ICT for record keeping.

2. **Lack of ICT Technicians and Personnel:** There is shortage of expertise that can handle the installation, operation and maintenance of ICT facilities. These areas are essential to the application of ICT to record keeping and management.

3. **Inadequate Funding/Financial Crisis:** Information and Communication Technology (ICT) facilities are not within the reach of the average Nigerian due to the high cost of acquiring them. This is posing a barrier to easy restricted individuals' access of these facilities for record keeping purposes. Financial resources form a key to the successful implementation and integration of ICT in record keeping and management. The current level of funding of education by the government and the decrease in budgetary allocation to the education sector is a major area of constraint to the provision of ICT facilities for record keeping and management.

4. **Lack of Basic Education and ICT Skills:**
This may pose a problem to record keeping since staff that ought to be using ICT facilities are not computer literate and, therefore, fail to maximally enjoy the benefits offered by ICT in record keeping and management. Also many of the academic and non- academic staff have conservative attitudes and still maintain their old ways of doing things and resist change.

5. **Unstable Power Supply:** Interruption of ICT facilities by electricity and computers network failure during record keeping.

6. Lack of interest among head teachers to adopt the use of ICT devices

Impact of ICT on Communication Process in Primary Schools

Communication may be defined as a "two-way process of convergence", in which information is shared by both parties and mutually beneficial relationships are forged between individuals, groups, and organizations, including schools and the families they serve Rogers (2003).Communication in school settings refers to dissemination of information, opinions and/ or ideas in order to enhance better understanding among the staff and the pupils/students which will in the same vein help towards achieving the goals for which the institution was established. Communication in schools is to maintain school culture and prepare tasks. Effective communication, which entails listening and responding as well as the frequent flow of quality information, is often cited as one of the most important determinants of successful collaboration between school and home.

Advanced ICTs can improve communication by providing new and more efficient ways in which

"Communications can be produced, distributed, displayed, and stored" Wright (2001). ICTs are transforming practices and changing expectations regarding school home communication. According to Pavlik (2007), these new technologies have a considerable influence on public relations. This suggests that choosing the appropriate communications technology is essential to maximize school and home communication efficacy and encourage familial involvement.

ICT Application on Parent –Teacher Relationship in Primary School

ICT could be used to engage parents and the community more actively. The aim is to create a learning community: parents could be offered ICT training, childcare facilities couldbe provided to facilitate attendance, and parent could be encouraged to provide laptops to students for home use. These types ICT initiatives could encourage students and parents to become involved with the school and with learning. Through these types of initiatives, vital information could be shared between parents and teachers as well as school management and the community via, e-mail and other online facilities much faster and convenient that you can ever imagined

Challenges of using ICT in Primary Schools

Challenges in the use of ICT in primary schools can be attributed to the following;

1. **Conservatism**: Some teachers have the feeling that change and use of ICT is not necessary and therefore, they may prefer the old ways of doing things. This slow down the pace of adoption of ICT.
2. **Availability**: Access to the computers made available to schools is restricted to a few staff for fear of misuse, theft or vandalization. For this reason, teachers keep away.
3. **Inadequate Manpower:** Raining facilities, services and employment of qualified people to man these centers are not available due to dearth of people with necessary skills.

4. **Electricity:** Most public primary schools do not have access to electricity which is a necessity for the use of ICT.

5. **Cost of ICT Facilities:** The cost aspect has led to a situation that most of the schools located in rural and semi-urban areas are yet to be provided with ICT centers.

6. **Technical Support:** ICT use was further limited by problems with technical support. In most schools, technical difficulties were reported as a major barrier to usage and a source of frustration for students and teachers. Also most schools where computers exist lacked permanent technical staff to solve these general maintenance and technical problems, so that computer teachers found themselves overwhelmed with this responsibility as well as teaching.

7. **Internet Connections:** Access to the Internet is of particular importance for schools. By providing access to the resources of the web, Internet access can facilitate learning activities centered on students' research. Most of the schools particularly the ones in rural communities don't have access to internet

CHAPTER FOUR

ICT AND THE MANAGEMENT OF SECONDARY SCHOOLS

Introduction

The role of technology in teaching and learning has become one of the most important and widely discussed issues in contemporary education engineering. Most experts in the field of education agreed that, when properly used, information and communication technology (ICT) hold great promise to improve teaching and learning in addition to shaping workforce opportunities. This has actually gingered a new and strong desire to equip schools with computer facilities and qualified personal necessary to produce technologically proficient and efficient students in developing countries like Nigeria. There is no doubt that computer can aid the instructional process and facilitate students' learning.

In Africa, concerted efforts have been made by many governments to initiate Internet connectivity and technology training programs. Such programs link schools around the world that in order to improve education, enhance cultural understanding and develop skills that youths need for securing jobs in the 21st century. In Uganda, an interconnectivity programme known as "Uganda School Net" is dedicated to extending educational technology throughout Uganda Carlson and Firpo(2001). In Senegal, teachers and students are using computers extensively as information tools. These programs in African countries mentioned are supported by their government through the ministries of Education. What is the Nigeria situation?

Need for ICT Application in Secondary Schools in Nigeria

Improved secondary education is essential to the creation of effective human capital in any country Evoh(2007). The need for ICT in Nigerian secondary schools cannot be overemphasized. In thistechnology-driven age, everyone requires ICT competence to survive. Organizations are finding it very necessary to train and re-train their employees to establish or increase their knowledge of computers and other ICT facilities Adomiand Anie(2006); This calls for early acquisition of ICT skills by many students)

ICT integration in secondary education needs to address management problems such as delays in decision making, communication barriers, time wasting and delay to complete tasks in the required time. The use of ICT within schools is an infusing aspect of school practices that benefit all staff and school activities at large. Computer can enhance educational efficiency. The efficiency in teaching various subjects could be improved. For instance, many secondary school teachers are already teaching large classes of students. In this situation, students no longer receive the much desired individual assistance. Furthermore, it is possible to use carefully prepared computer programs to ensure that learners are accurately and systematically instructed.

1. The ability to use computers effectively has become an essential part of everyone's education. Skills such as bookkeeping, clerical and administrative work, stocktaking, and so forth, now constitute a set of computerized practices that form the core IT skills package: spreadsheets, word processors, and databases (Reffell and Whitworth, 2002).

2. There are developments in the Nigerian education sector which indicate some level of ICT application in the secondary schools. The Federal Government of Nigeria, in the National Policy on Education(Federal Republic of Nigeria, 2004), recognizes the prominent role of ICTs in the modern world, and has integrated ICTs into education in Nigeria. To actualize this goal, the document states that government will provide basic infrastructure and training at the primary school. At the junior secondary school, computer education has been made a pre-vocational elective, and is a vocational elective at the senior secondary school. It is also the intention of government to provide necessary infrastructure and training for the integration of ICTs in the secondary school system.

3. New instructional techniques that use ICTs provide a different modality of instruments. For the students, ICT use allows for increased individualization of learning. In schools where new technologies are used, students have access to tools that adjust to their attention span and provide valuable and immediate feedback for literacy

enhancement, which is currently almost taking over the sphere of our educational system in Nigerian.

4. Nigerian society need intellectual and creative employees who's novel ideas are to a certain extend a guarantee of society's' existence. Contemporary society strongly needs highly able minds that could productively solve many economic problems of today. Such highly able minds are nurtured by a country's educational institutions

5. Modern society desperately needs highly able citizens who can bring innovative solutions to its current challenges and at the same time produce new ideas for ongoing socio-economic and political advancement

ICT and Administrative Work in Secondary Schools

Computers can serve administrative functions. They can replace the laborious exercise of filing papers in filing cabinets and shelves where records accumulate dust over a long period of time. Another administrative application of the computers is their use for;

1. Budget planning
2. Accounting for expenditure
3. Writing correspondences and reports
4. Assigning students to classes
5. Reporting students' progress
6. Testing students
7. Scoring tests which help to reduce paper work.
8. Sending e-mail notices and agendas to staff, rather than printing and distributing them
9. Submission of lesson plans through e-mail
10. Insist that all teachers create a class Web page

It is true that many of the tasks above are not effectively and efficiently done in secondary schools in Nigeria. School effectiveness is a goal set by administrative leaders and their leadership strategies to help the school reach certain achievements across the board. Using ICT applications in school management will help in achieving the stated objective easily. The teachers tend to do well in term of teaching and learning using ICT application and the students tend to do well by constantly practicing.

Factors Hindering ICT Application in Secondary Schools

Several factors are attributed to low ICT application in secondary schools in Nigeria. Some of these factors are but not limited to the following:

1. **Poor Information Infrastructure**: In Nigeria, a formidable obstacle to the use of information and communication technology is infrastructure deficiencies. Computer equipment was made to function with other infrastructure such as electricity under "controlled conditions". Currently, there is no part of the country, which can boast of electricity supply for 24 hours a day except probably areas where government officials live. This has deny secondary schools the opportunity to benefit from the use of electronic equipment such as radio, television, video recorders, and computers among others. The few Internet access available in Nigeria is found in city centres' (Aduwa &Iyamu, 2005).

2. **Inadequate ICT Facilities in Schools:** Another obstacle to ICT development in Nigeria schools is inadequate

telecommunication facilities. Most school don't have not to talk of not been enough

3. **Frequent Electricity Interruption:** Electronics equipment such as radio, television, video recorder and even computers has been damaged due to irregular power supply. When electricity supply is not stable and constant, it is difficult to keep high-tech equipment such as computers functioning, especially under extreme weather conditions as obtained in Nigeria.

4. **Non-availability of Electricity Supply:** Most secondary schools located in rural communities do not have access to electricity supply, even in urban areas, there are cases of secondary schools without electricity. In such instance, the use of ICT can only be imagined. This indeed does not argue well for the well being of the students and the school in particular.

5. **Poor ICT Policy/project Implementation Strategy:** The Nigerian Federal Government's 1988 policy introduced computer education to the high schools Okebukola, (1997). The only way this policy was implemented was the distribution of computers to federal government high schools, which were never used for computer education of the students. No effort was made to distribute computer to state government or private schools. Although the government planned to integrate ICTs into the school system and provide schools with infrastructure, concerted efforts have not. been made to provide facilities and trained personnel. Thus, most schools do not yet offer ICT training programmes (Goshit, 2006)

6. **High cost of ICT Facilities/Components:**The price of computer hardware and software continues to drop in most developed countries, but in developing countries,

such as Nigeria, the cost of computers is several times more expensive. Apart from the basic computers themselves, other costs associated with peripherals such as printers, monitors, paper, modem, extra disk drives are beyond the reach of most secondary schools in Nigeria. The schools cannot also afford the exorbitant Internet connection fees

7. **Non integration ICT into the school curriculum:** There is no doubt that the ultimate power of technology is the content and the communication. Though, software developers and publishers in Nigeria have been trying for long to develop software and multimedia that have universal application, due to the differences in education standards and requirements, these products do not integrate into curriculum across country.

8. **Inadequate ICT manpower in the schools:** There is acute shortage of trained personnel in application software, operating systems, network administration and local technicians to service and repair computer facilities. Those who are designated to use computers in Nigeria do not receive adequate training.

9. **Limited ICT skills Among Teachers:** Nigeria secondary schools does not only experience inadequate information infrastructure, it also has issues of deficiency in human skills and knowledge on the part of the teachers to fully integrate ICT into secondary education. Most secondary school teachers lack the skills to fully utilize technology in curriculum implementation hence the traditional chalk and duster approach still dominates in secondary school pedagogy To use information and communication technology (ICT) in secondary schools in Nigeria, the

need for adequately trained teachers to install, maintain and support these systems cannot be over emphasized.

10. **Poor perception of ICT among Teachers and Administrators:** Teachers are afraid of being embarrassed if they do not know how to operate a sudden stuck computers, Teachers also may be afraid of being replaced by computers, Teachers may perceive that by using machine in their teaching, the teaching process will be too mechanized, everything will be strictly controlled and depend on computers/machines.

11. **Location of school:** In rural Nigeria most inhabitant do not have access to electricity, thereby denying rural secondary schools opportunity to benefit from the use of electronic equipment such as radio, television, video recorders and computers. The few Internet access available in Nigeria is found in urban centers. These environmental realities are difficult to manage because fans, sealed rooms and stable electricity are lacking in many urban homes and rural areas.

12. **Inadequate Educational Software:** Software that is appropriate and culturally suitable to the Nigerian education system is in short supply. There is a great discrepancy between relevant software supply and demand in developing countries like Nigeria. Even if Nigeria tries to approach this software famine by producing software that would suit its educational philosophies; there are two major problems to be encountered. First, the cost of producing relevant software for the country's educational system is enormous. Second, there is dearth of qualified computer software designers in the country(Samuel and Ede, 2005)

Administrative Roles of Principals in ICT Management

Improved secondary education is essential to the creation of effective human capital in any country. The need for ICT in Nigerian secondary schools cannot be overemphasized. The ability to use computers effectively has become an essential part of everyone's education.Skills such as bookkeeping, clerical and administrative work, stocktaking, and so forth, now constitute aset of computerized practices that form the core IT skills package used in secondary schools today(Evoh, 2007).

The importance of ICT contribution is also widely recognized by school administrators. It has become a vital enabling tool that can no longer be ignored in the management of schools. However, strategies must be put in place school managers to enhance ICT use in the delivery of management services in public secondary schools. The principals must therefore come to terms with the really of the 21st century by creating avenues and proving enabling environment for effective utilization of ICTs in the schools. It will be an impossible task to plan and administer any school in which records are not kept or are carelessly and fraudulently kept. Educational administrators need to have adequate and accurate data of students' enrolment and school personnel records for effective planning and management of schools.

One cannot over-estimate the utilization of ICT in everyday activities of the school, when principals do the needful; ICT will assist them to meet the task of school management in the areas of;

1. curriculum and instruction,
2. school community relationship
3. school business operations,

4. daily school routine,
5. school programmes and services,
6. solving individuals or groups' problems, and
7. as well as staff development.

In line with this assertion, Gronow (2007) noted that, the Principal's delegation of an ICT leader promotes the personal belief in the importance of ICT in the school. The ICT leader as the expert supplies the Principal with advice on ICT. The Principal, with the support of the ICT leader and school community, can develop an ICT vision and e- learning plan, aimed at developing a sustainable direction for ICT in teaching and learning, administration and business of the school organization.

It was also noted that when ICT is effectively managed, it will present new opportunities for teaching and learning, and enhancing school management by providing for teacher-to-learners, teacher-to-teacher and learner-to-learner communication and cooperation, enhanced opportunities for several technologies delivered by teachers, creating superior keenness for learning among students and for effective and efficient management.

Specific Roles of Principals in ICT Management

1. Ensure accurate records of available ICT facilities in school are properly kept
2. Developing realistic and practicable policy on the utilization and a maintenance of such facilities
3. Ensuring that experts are assigned the control and coordination of ICT activities in the school

4. Ensuring that both teachers and students are properly oriented on the need to key into the use of ICT in the process of teaching and learning.
5. Providing good organizational climate in the school to foster peaceful co-existence

In education, in particular, ICT is a tool for transforming the education setting. However, transformation is only successful where there are effective change management strategies and appropriate leadership. At the school level, rapid changes need to be effected in order to change the role that principals take particularly in relation to leading the change process.

CHAPTER FIVE

ICT AND THE MANAGEMENT OF TERTIARY INSTITUTIONS

Introduction

In a rapidly changing world of global market competition, automation, and increasing democratization, higher education is necessary for an individual to have the capacity and capability to access and apply information. Such ability and capability must find bearing in information and communication technology in the global village. The Economic Commission for Africa has indicated that the ability to access and effectively utilize information is no longer a luxury but a necessity for development. Unfortunately, many developing countries, especially in Africa, are already on the wrong side of the digital divide in the educational use of ICT.

Higher education around the world is facing unprecedented changes. As these changes continue to accelerate the various higher institutions are subjected to external and internal pressures from stakeholders and students. Major reforms in higher institutions have recognized the changing nature in higher education and the need for change at both the institutional and individual level to make them more mobile, synergetic, creative, future-oriented and sustainable. Higher education should be anticipatory to social, economic and cultural life as well as form desirable sustainable future.

It is not uncommon to find that many establishments in Nigeria, including educational institutions, still keep records in files and tucked them away in filling cabinets where they accumulate dust. A great deal of routine administrative work in government establishment is still done manually with the state and the Federal government showing little or no interest in embracing ICT. If Nigerian wants to be a major player in the global market place of ideas and prepare her citizens for the new environment of today and the future, the country should embrace ICT for the following reasons: ICT as aids to teaching and learning; ICT as a tool for management; ICT as instrument for economic development; ICT as instrument of high technological development, and ICT as a course of study.

The success of ICT in higher institutions will depend largely, on attitude of lecturers and their willingness to embrace it in discharging their functions appropriately, especially in the age of globalization. Hence it is important that to integrate ICT in the management of higher education to reflect on teaching/learning situation, research and administrative functions.

Role of ICT in Institutional Administration

Administration is a process of planning activities and utilizing human and imperial resources with an aim of accomplishing of goals and objectives of a particular organization or institution. It calls for the ability of the administrators to make the right decisions at the right time to fulfill the predetermined goals. In educational institutional setting therefore, administration has been extended as a service activity or tool through which the fundamental objectives of the institutional process may be optimized more efficiently when allocating human and material resources as well as making the best use of existing resources (Opara&Onyije, 2014).

In the words of Opara andOnyije(2014) Information and Communication Technology in Educational Administration are facilities, tools or resources that could be used to process, store,preserve, access, retrieve, and disseminate information with ease. It could be seen as the engine for growth and tool for empowerment, with profound implications for education, change, and socio-economic development, the dream of any institution is an effective and efficient managerial process to accomplish their needs and goals. The knowledge of computer application software such as spreadsheet, computer aided design, and databases are important skills in institutional administration.

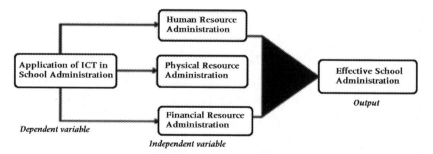

Figure 1: Application of ICT in School Administration. Adopted from Jacinta (2014)

There are several uses of ICT in Administration of Higher Institutions of Learning:

1. ICT can increase school efficiency and reduce unnecessary bureaucracy in school administration.
2. With ICT, the administrators can discharge their duties by using computers and Internet in solving school problems at hand and in carrying out their day-to-day assignment especially as it relates to having a reliable information system.
3. ICT can play a major role in reducing the work load of the administrators and staff especially in analyzing information like analyzing student academic performance hence much time is saved.
4. ICT also helps in managing student admission, student records and examination records.
5. The monitoring and evaluation of staff, planning for school activities, curriculum development, financial management and information dissemination, promotes communication between school units, parents, and principal administration (Oboegbulem&Ugwu, 2013).

Liverpool & Jacinta (2013) outlined the role of ICT in Institutional Administration:

1. **Organisation of Information:** Institution administrators need to have basic information on students and lecturer flows. For example, categorizes data on student/staff by sex, level, state of origin, performance in schools etc. They could used Microsoft Access or Excel to organize data into an easily accessible format and can be easily stored and retrieved from the micro computer.
2. **Computation and Processing of Paper Work:** ICT are used to map out different activities of the academic session such as number of weeks for teaching, conducting

of continuous assessment tests, examination periods and when the result could be released to students. Others activities such as stipulated time for teaching practice and student industrial work experience scheme (SIWES). Institutional administrator could use Microsoft Access, Excel or other simple applications to collect and keeps records of events, enhancement of effective happening in the institution, issues out notices of meeting for staff, students and parents.

3. **Enhancement of Effective Communication:** With the installation of computers and internets communication made it easier for the institutional administrator to use telephone, fax and other communication facilities for transforming thoughts, sharing and imparting of information, growing and receiving and understanding of message within a network of independent relationship across international frontiers.

4. **Enhancement of Planning:** Institutional administrator could use ICT to plan and make decisions on the basis of accurate and readily available facts. ICT could be use to plan the budgets of the college expenditure and plans for replacement of both obsolete and repairs of broken down equipment or institutional facilities.

5. **Improvement of Monitoring:** Institutional administrators use microcomputers in monitoring various areas in the institutional system, such as the uses of continuous monitoring and assessment of students learning and achievement in the institution. Campbell and Sellburn (2002) pointed out that ICT can be valuable for storing and analyzing data on education indicators, students' assessments, educational, human and material resources and cost and finance.

6. **Managed Instruction:** This is an approach by the institutional administrators to use computer in scheduling courses/subjects, space, installation, inventory and personnel control, recording and reporting attendance, school accounting, storage and retrieval of student information marks management. This is capable of generating the demographic data of students and institutional staff, production of results online.

Benefits of ICT as Learning and Teaching Resource

1. Make students to become independent learners and good beginners.
2. Help to increase students' writing skills
3. Help to present information in many forms
4. Make learners' to be more confident in learning process
5. Communicates effectively on any process
6. Give reason to greater problem solving and critical thinking.
7. Develop in the students the spirit to interact with their fellow students.
8. Help student to work collaboratively(Kosakowaski, 2005).

ICT and Educational Governance in Tertiary Institutions

Information is a critical resource in the operation and management of tertiary institutions. Timely availability of relevant information is vital for effective performance of managerial functions such as planning, organizing, leading and control. An information system in tertiary institution is like the nervous system in the human body; it is the link that connects all the tertiary institution components e.g personnel, admission, exams and record, bursary, library, sickbay, student's affaire unit, security and management unit.

The use of ICT in educational management will aid analyzing data quickly and accurately quick, decision making, provides power to Administrators for efficient management of education and institution, reduces the burden of Teachers, available at lowest total cost of ownership, provides information at the door steps and reduces the Right to Information Applications. The crucial role of ICT in managing higher education and stimulating sustainable development is twofold. While it allows institutions to leapfrog stages of institutional growth by being able to modernize their production system and value system, it also bring about retardation to those institutions that are unable to adapt to the new technological system

A very important part of Information administration is general administration of higher education institutions which includes the various day-to-day activities of the entire system. Through literature reviews, it is evident that the integration of ICT into general administration has brought increased efficiency and optimal resource utilization Hasan(2007). The various items classified under this category include usage of electronic media for scheduling of halls and other resources, fee payment, and handling internal and external examination activities in coordination with the school members, all day to-day activities, intra and inter communication etc.

The dream of any institution in an effective and efficient managerial process is to accomplish their needs and goals. OhakweandOkwuanaso (2006) contended that the knowledge of computer application software's such as spreadsheet, excel, computer-aided design and database are important skills which enables institutional administrators in processing relevant data for the governing bodies, institutional agencies for decision making towards quality assurance and transformational development.

Iwu& Ike (2009) categorized the use of ICT for effective and efficient governance of tertiary institutions as follows:

1. **Sensing Technologies:** These equipment gather data and translate them into form that can be understood by the computer, such as scanners, sensors, keyboard, mouse, electronic pen, barcode sensors or readers, touch of digital boards, voice recognition system etc. Institutional administrators could use them for computation and processing of paper work. These sensory technologies gather data to do complex computation very rapidly and accurately. Similarly, institutional administrator could use word processing to draft, revise and produce reports of high quality for presentation without much hard labour, frustration and waste of time.

2. **Communication Technologies:** These are equipment that institutional administrators could use to transfer information from the sources to users. They are capable of overcoming natural barriers to information transfer like speed and distance. These include; facsimile machines (fax), telephone, electronic mail, telecommunication system, teleconferencing, electronic bulletin boards etc.

3. **Display Technologies:** These are output devices that form the interface between sensing, communication and analyzing technologies and human user. These include; computer screen, printers, television etc. Every computer in the institution has to be connected to the internet. The office of the institutional administrators is open

to the public, to researchers, staff, students and parents wanting information about the institution. They can find all of that information on the internet. This makes the work easier by reducing the flow of people through the office and improves access to information.

4. **Analysis Technologies:** These are the technologies that help the institutional administrator to investigate of query of data, analysis and in-depth query for answers from simple to complex phenomena in administrative procedures. ICT has changed the way in which institutional administrators collect and analyze data. For instance, the use of Access, excel and other simple applications to collect, store and analyze information. They may also need some sophisticated packages like SPSS (statistical package for the social science). This is to improve the timeliness and volume of information in implementing an institutional management information system.

5. **Storage Technologies:** These technologies facilitate the efficient and effective storage of information in a form that can be easily accessed. They include: magnetic tapes, disks, optical disks, cassettes, flash drive, memory card, zip drive etc

Other uses of ICT for educational governance in higher institutions include:

1. ICT technology can process voluminous records quickly, meticulously and impeccably.
2. Technology can generate reliable and consistent records.
3. Records and data produced are searchable and quickly retrievable.

4. Digital records save space, a premium cost to institutions.

5. Technology saves human resources for data entry and servicing student admission and registration.

6. With advanced scanning technology, completed application forms can be read into the databases in a matter of seconds.

7. Other software like Learning Management Systems (LMS) e.g., the open source Moodle allow students to register for courses directly online, pay online and get course information online.

8. Technology can expand the geographical boundary for student intake and facilitate cross-border higher education.

9. Using ICT in higher education administration is fundamentally about harnessing technology for better planning, setting standards, effecting change and monitoring results of the core functions of universities (Krishnaveni&Meenakumari, 2010).

ICT as aid to Teaching and Learning

ICT provides a platform for new initiatives. This can be achieved when tertiary institutionsfocus on new initiatives through transitions and transformation of higher education curricula, structure and management. The role of ICT in higher education in Nigeria cannot be over emphasized.

Apart from its use in the classroom for teaching/learning, it enhancescurriculum content and teaching methods of teachers. Research developmentand other out –of classroom activities are not left out. In recent times, ICT isused in the management of staff from recruitment to retirement and studentsfrom screening, registration to graduation.

The use of ICT by academics in most universities is low. This further confirm the assertion that in spiteof the tremendous use of ICT facilities in teaching-learning situation, the state of ICT facilities in Nigeria's higher institutions is not too challenging and exploiting ICT potentials for educational use is on the worrying side. Akpan(2008) corroborating this assertion confirm that lecturers recognize the importance of ICT in teaching and learning but their competence and usage of the available ICT facilities is below expectations. It is therefore evident that teacher's attitude towards ICT affect the successful use of ICT in institutions. This attitude could be indifferent dimensions namely: Affective Domain, Behaviour Intentions,Perceived Usefulness and Perceived Competence level, and Knowledge of ICT.

It is evident that lecturer attitudes towards ICT usage are predictor for future classroom useand development Myers and Halpin, (2002). Sequel to this, Olisaemeka and Onwusoanya (2009) noted that there are strong expectations and political pressures on the educational system to increase the use of Information and Communication Technologies (ICTs) to enhance performance and facilities flexibility in education. Consequently, ICTs are used for teaching and integrating learning across the curriculum, meaning that availability of ICT devices and a conducive climate will enable students and their lecturers to access and evolve effective learning and effective administration. ICT status in Nigerian higher institutions revealed that there is a big gap in ICT skills between the average Nigerian students and academic staff compared to other institutions around the globe. According to him, if this gap is not addressed with immediate Intervention of ICT adoption processes, will continue to grow far beyond the present situation (Aniebonam, 2007).

Access to ICT is an essential factor in the development of higher education for sustainable development. Knowledge of ICT will go a long way to enhance both lecturers and students ability in their academic work, improve their acquisition of basic employable skills, solve some basic academic and societal problems through research and contribute positively towards sustainable development in the society.

ICT and Financial Transactions in Tertiary Institutions

Application of ICT in financial transactions made by the school helps in creating transparency. This prevents most of the school administrators from misusing the financial resources that are available in the school and thus channeling the resources to their appropriate designations. The increase in transparency in the financial management referred to by the World Bank is one of the central elements in the assumed democratizing role of ICTs.

This greater transparency would have been possible by means of two factors which usually characterize the digital revolution, and a third aspect far less explained Almiron(2007). ICT application has efficient and safer ways of carrying out financial transactions over a short period of time. School administrators can adopt the use of ICT in paying of their staff members, making orders for school supply Cheryl (2005). This enables the school administration to be able to keep record of all the transactions done. Thus they are able to gauge themselves on the basis of the amount spend and the amount received. This in turn gives the school administrators a chance to gauge how sustainable they are in terms of finance.

Use of ICT enables schools to take advantage of electronic banking which allows them to check their bank account records in real time, saving time and helping ensure that payments due have been made and received, and also to operate the bank account within any agreed overdraft limit. Large and overseas payments can be made quickly and securely with on-line banking, as long as the school has its own security checks to protect against theft by staff or by anyone else who managed to obtain account details and passwords (Grey,2000).

ICT Application on Provision of Support Services in Tertiary Institutions

The student services concept is used to describe the divisions or departments which provide services and student support in higher education. Its purpose is to ensure the students growth and development during the academic experience NASPA (2102). Amid increasing diversity of students admitted to tertiary institutions, there has evolved additional support services that have contributed to the academic and personal development of students, including academic skills development programs and specific support to students who have difficulty learning or adapting to university life. Such services contribute to the quality of the academic experience and help students to achieve learning potential.

The functioning and organization pattern of student services varies from country to country. In some countries these services are part of university management (integrated into a student services department) in others, such as France, they are outsourced to specialized organizations. Student services are seen as key components of many academic systems. Mass recruitment into higher education has diversified student populations. In developing countries for example, students from disadvantaged groups, women, rural youth and ethnic or religious minorities have now the opportunity to study at a higher level. The student's continuing concern is therefore necessary to ensure success in current higher education (Alina, 2013).

An important role of student services is *to prepare students for active participation in society.* Along with teachers and non-governmental organizations they contribute to increased learning opportunities and community involvement by organizing or promoting internships, experiential units or short-term experiences, integrated into the curricula. (UNESCO, 2002). Among the services available to students, the most important are those which meet their *academic, personal development and emotional needs* (McInnis, 2004)

ICT and Admission Process in Tertiary Institutions

Student administration is an important and integral part of information administration. This involves various activities commencing from the admission process to learning activities till processing of results and performance analysis. The integration of ICT into this process enhances the overall admission activities of higher education institutions by making it more accessible to many (Thomas, 2004). The important item identified under this category relates to the automation of admission process through e-media. This includes admission enquiry by students, applying for admissions through electronic media, registration / enrolment using computers, course allotment, and availability of information like timetable / class schedule in electronic form and attendance monitoring / maintenance through e-media. Further it includes the various communications relating to transport, hostel accommodation and other communication to guardians/parents. The integration also helps in expansion of the geographical boundaries for student intake, thus facilitating cross-border higher education.

ICT and Information Dissemination in Tertiary Institutions

Christiana (2008) opined that ICT fosters the dissemination of information and knowledge by separating content from its physical location. This flow of information is largely impervious to geographic boundaries allowing remote communities to become integrated into global networks and making information, knowledge and culture accessible, in theory, to anyone. It is also mentioned that ICT enhances day-to-day management of institutions and the various functional areas in which it could be used are specified below:

1. Timetabling
2. Student admission and Tracking
3. Financial Management
4. Medical services
5. Procurement and Store management
6. Data distribution and management

In general, a good communication system should also be in place for the overall effectiveness of administration. ICT helps in providing a good communication system in higher education system Magni (2009). ICT helps in providing timely information to all concerned. Communication could be for internal and external information acquisition and dissemination. It includes communication between the important stakeholders of the system such as sending e-circulars to students, school and staff. The dissemination of information about the institution using e-kiosks is also a very important item to be considered.

ICT and Security of Information in Tertiary Institutions

The term information security is related to the following basic concepts: Confidentiality, Integrity, and Availability (CIA).The confidentiality, integrity and availability of security is a general concept for a secure ICT system. ICTs have a transversal use in schools, covering the various academic and non-academic teaching activities in their various aspects: curricular, teaching, recreational and administrative tasks. In school activities, students are stimulated to use ICTs to research, present and publish project works, to communicate and interact,(Host land, 2010)

In the words of Quigley, (2011), Protection of information has been a major challenge since the beginning of the computer age. Given the widespread adoption of computer technology for both business and academic operations, the problem of information protection has become more urgent than ever. Computer files, databases, networking and the Internet based applications all have gradually become part of the most critical assets of an organization. When these assets are attacked, damaged or threatened, data integrity becomes an issue and the proper operation of the organization may be interrupted.

Academic Institutions tend to have formulated ICT policies, which among things address security concerns. Such institutions make use of Encryption System. Encrypting such files at least helps protect institutions with physical security measures, digital rights management systems which prevent unauthorized use. Access Control Systems to control access to information and computer systems, the aim is to define a set of account management standards that will restrict access to authorized personnel and safeguard the services and information. This is done mostly by use of passwords.

Other existing protection methods are; Active Content Monitoring but the most frequent is the Antivirus, interior and exterior firewall and central backup servers. There is, however a limited number of Institutions protecting themselves to this level, this is mainly because of the costs involved. Most of the software protection available involves regular renewal of licenses and subscriptions, and these costs are considered.

The purpose of information security is to protect an organization's valuable resources, such as information, hardware, and software. Through the selection and application of appropriate safeguards, security helps the organization's mission by protecting its physical and financial resources, reputation, legal position, employees, another tangible and intangible assets (Harisinh, 2008).

Gunnar, Per Arne (2011); assert that ICT security architecture for the Higher Education sector must meet the following overall requirements:

1. Institutions must provide adequate protection for their information assets. Security and risk levels must be well-established at the management level and based on risk assessments.
2. The ICT systems must comply with the institution's information security policy.
3. Consideration must be given to relevant regulatory requirements and directives, such as the government policy on ICT local legislation.
4. The security architecture must comply with the institution's objectives as stipulated in [appropriate local legislation], and with any agreements the institution may have with third parties.

5. The ICT systems must be equipped with appropriate capacity and adequate robustness in the event of failure (resilience).

6. The ICT systems must have sufficient quality.

ICT and Decision Making Process in Tertiary Institutions

There are increasing societal demands on Nigerian modern educational institutions for good results in terms of the functionality of the type of education given. University education in particular is looked upon for meeting the manpower needs of the country. Thus, universities are complex organizations with multiple goals which are accomplished through their major roles of teaching, research and community service (FRN, 2004).

The more complex an organization's structure is, the greater the need for coordination within and between sections and departments. However, central to the needed coordination is information. Infact, the information needed for effective decision making in universities cannot be provided from people's often deficient memories. Therefore, a university needs a system that creates knowledge, stores the knowledge so created and established to ensure continuity of thought, reason and adaptive academic pursuit; and recall at will and disseminate the stored knowledge or information for use in taking decisions which are in the interest of the society at large (Adedipe, 1995; Alabi and Akinnubi, 2013).

In education system, decision-making is the process of selecting the appropriate action(s) to be taken which aimed at improving the well-being of the educational institutions. In the opinion of Ocheni, (2015) educational system is expanding at an unprecedented rate because it appears that the demand for appropriate, adequate and timely information for management decisions in Nigerian educational institutions is challenging. The educational planners, administrators and policy makers need more than ever before accurate, up-to-date and timely information to make appropriate decisions. Right decisions give direction for a right course of action. Ocheni, (2015) stated that when an organization is designed to provide correct information to managers, decision making processes work extremely well and tasks will be accomplished. However, when information is poorly designed, problem-solving and decision making processes will be ineffective and managers may not understand why and this could create inefficiency in the administrative processes.

Areas that need Relevant and Timely Information for Effective Decision Making in Tertiary Institutions are as Follows:

1. Demographic data on potential secondary education output
2. Student population, composition, socio-economic background, male/female ratio, assessment of academic progress
3. Staff categories, salaries, workloads, evaluation, updating of knowledge
4. Accounting data, both for planning and operational purposes
5. Data for evaluation of curricula and teaching methods
6. Utilization and relative utility value of services such as material resources and student welfare services(Alabi and Akinnubi, 2013)

Challenges of using ICT Facilities in Tertiary Institutions

High telecommunication costs, infrastructure, inadequate human resources and sustainability of new projects policy and funding issues are part of the challenges facing the integration of ICT in higher education in Nigeria Munyua, (2000); Johnson, (2006).

However in specific terms, Esoswo (2011) suggested the following as serious challenges to the use of ICT in tertiary institutions;

1. **Infrastructure Related Challenges:** A country's educational technology infrastructure sits on top of the national telecommunications and information infrastructure. Before any ICT-based programme is launched, policymakers and planners must carefully consider the following: In the first place, are there appropriate rooms or buildings available to house the technology? In countries where there are many old school buildings, extensive retrofitting to ensure proper electrical wiring, heating/cooling and ventilation, and safety and security would be needed.

Another basic requirement is the availability of electricity and telephony. Indeveloping countries large areas are still without a reliable supply of electricity. For instance, a basic requirement for computer-based or online learning is access to computers in schools, communities, and households, as well as affordable Internet service which is seriously lacking.

2. **Capacity Building Challenges:** MacDougall and Squires (1997) noted that there are various competencies that

must be developed throughout the educational system for ICT integration to be successful.

1. **Teachers**: Teacher professional development should have five focuses.

    a) Skills with particular applications;
    b) Integration into existing curricula;
    c) Curricular changes related to the use of IT (including changes in instructional design);
    d) Changes in teacher role; and
    e) Underpinning educational theories.

Research -on the use of ICTs in different educational settings over the years invariably identify as a barrier to success shows the inability of teachers to understand why they should use ICTs and how exactly they can use ICTs to help them teach better. Unfortunately, most teacher professional development in ICTs is heavy on "teaching the tools" and light on "using the tools to teach.

2. **Education Administrators**: Leadership plays a key role in ICT integration in education. Many teacher- or student-initiated ICT projects have been undermined by lack of support from education administrators. For ICT integration programs to be effective and sustainable, administrators themselves must be competent in the use of the technology, and they must have a broad understanding of the technical, curricular, administrative, financial, and social dimensions of ICT use in education

3. **Technical Support Specialists**: Whether provided by in-school staff or external service providers, or

both, technical support specialists are essential to the continued viability of ICT use in a given school. While the technical support requirements of an institution depend ultimately on what and how technology is deployed and used, general competencies that are required would be in the installation, operation, and maintenance of technical equipment (including software), network administration, and network security. Without on-site technical support, much time and money may be lost due to technical breakdowns.

4. **Content Developers:** Content development is a critical area that is too often overlooked. The bulk of existing ICT-based educational material is likely to be in English or of little relevance to education in developing countries (especially at the primary and secondary levels). There is a need to develop original educational content (e.g., radio programs, interactive multimedia learning materials on CDROM or DVD, Web-based courses, etc.), adapt existing content, and convert print based content to digital media. These are tasks for which content development specialists such as instructional designers, scriptwriters, audio and video production specialists, programmers, multimedia course authors, and web developers are needed.

3. **Challenges Related to Financing the Cost of ICT Use:** One of the greatest challenges in ICT use in education is balancing educational goals with economic realities. ICTs in education programs require large capital investments and developing countries need to be prudent

in making decisions about what models of ICT use will be introduced and to be conscious of maintaining economies of scale. Ultimately it is an issue of whether the value-added of ICT use offsets the cost, relative to the cost of alternatives. Put another way, is ICT-based learning the most effective strategy for achieving the desired educational goals, and if so what is the modality and scale of implementation that can be supported given existing financial, human and other resources?

Whyte as cited by Cisler (2002) suggested the following potential sources of money and resources for ICT use programs:

1. Grants
2. Public subsidies
3. Private donations, fund-raising events
4. In-kind support (e.g., equipment, volunteers)
5. Community support (e.g. rent-free building)
6. Membership fees
7. Revenues earned from core business:
8. Connectivity (phone, fax, Internet, web pages)
9. Direct computer access to user
10. Office services (photocopying, scanning, audiovisual aids
11. Revenues earned from ancillary activities:
12. Business services (word-processing, spreadsheets, budget preparation,
13. printing, reception services)
14. Educational services (distant education, training courses)
15. Community services (meeting rooms, social events, local information,
16. remittances from migrant workers)

Ilaonisi and Osuagwu (2010) indicated that many factors limit the infusion of ICTin educational institutions in Nigeria. These include;

1. paucity of ICT infrastructure and lack of access;
2. high enrolments,
3. inadequate funding;
4. absence of funding allocation to technology;
5. high cost of ownership and cost to the consumer;
6. unsteady and Inadequate Electrical Power Supply

REFERENCES

Adedipe, N.O. (1995). University management constraints and stresses: A personal experience. *Text of a keynote address at the 1995 MIS national seminar organised by NUC.*

Adomi, E.E. (2005a). Internet development and connectivity in Nigeria.*Program 39* (3): 257-68.

Adomi, E.E. (2005b). The effects of a price increase on cybercafé services in Abraka, Nigeria. *TheBottom Line: Managing Library Finances 18* (2): 78-86.

Aginam, E. (2006). NEPAD scores students' ICT education in Africa Low. *Vanguard.*Available: http://www.vanguardngr. com/articles/2002/features/technology/tec527092006.html .

Akbaba-Altun, S. (2006).Complexity of integrating computer technologies in education in Turkey.*Educational Technology and Society, 9*(1), 176-187.

Akpan, C. P. (2008). Lecturers' perception of the role of ICT in the management of University Education for sustainable development in Nigeria.*Nigeria Journal of Education Administration and planning.* 8(1) 113-127.

Alabi, A. T. &Akinnubi, O. P. (2013) ICT and Decision Making in Universities in North-CentralGeo-Political Zone, Nigeria

Alexander, J.O. (1999). Collaborative design, constructivist learning, information technology immersion, & electronic communities: a case study. *Interpersonal Computing and Technology*: An Electronic Journal for the 21st Century No.7, Pp; 1–2.

Almiron-Roig, N. (2007). ICTs and financial crime: an innocent fraud? *International Communication Gazette*, Volume 69, number 1, February 2007.

Aniebonam, C. M. (2007).Using technology to drive education reforms inNigeria.*E-Journal of Nigerian IT Professionals in the Americas*.Availableat: www.nitpa.orh.

Alan, D. G. (2009).Mapping the Latest Research into Video-Based Distance Education.*Wainhouse Research LLC*, USA,

Anderson, T. (2004).*Theory and practice of online learning*. Athabasca, AB: Athabasca University.

Attwell, P; Battle, J. (1999)."Home Computers and School Performance".*The Information Society*. No. (15), Pp. 1-10.

Barron, A. (1998). Designing Web-based training. *British Journal of Educational Technology*, **Vol.** 29, No. (4), Pp; 355-371.

Becker, H. J. (2000). "Pedagogical Motivations for Student Computer Use that Leads to Student Engagement".*Education Technology*.**Vol.** 40, No. 5, Pp; 5-17.

Berge, Z. (1998). Guiding principles in Web-based instructional design.*Education Media International,* **Vol.** 35No.(2), Pp;72-76.

Bhattacharya, I. & Sharma, K. (2007), 'India in the knowledge economy – an electronic paradigm', *International Journal of Educational Management* **Vol**. 21 No. 6, Pp. 543- 568.

Bottino, R. M. (2003),'ICT, national policies, and impact on schools and teachers' development''CRPIT '03: Proceedings of the 3.1 and 3.3 working groups conference on *International federation for information processing'*, *Australian Computer Society,* Inc., Darlinghurst, Australia, Australia, 3-6.

Bransford, J. D., Sherwood, R. D., Hassel bring, T. S., Kinzer, C. K., & Williams, S. M. (1990). Anchored instruction: why we need it and how technology can help. In D. Nix & R. Spiro 10 (Eds.), *Cognition, education, multimedia Exploring ideas in high technology* (Pp. 115–141). Hillsdale, NJ: Lawrence Erlbaum Associates.

Chandra, S. &Patkar, V. (2007), 'ICTS: A catalyst for enriching the learning process and library services in India', The International Information & Library Review **Vol**. 39, No. (1), Pp; 1-11.

Cisler, S. (2002).*Planning for Sustainability: How to keep your ICT Project Running*. Retrieved April 23, 2011, from http// www. cid.harvard. edu/cr/pdf/gitrr2 002_chO4 pdf

Cheryl, H. W. (2005). *Educational technologists in Higher Education Institutions in South Africa*: Moving beyond random acts of progress. 355-361.

Christiana, M. (2008).Information and Communication Technology for Administration andManagement for secondary schools in Cyprus.*Journal of Online Learning and Teaching 4(3)*. Retrieved on January 12, 2015 at: http://www.academia.edu/6317337/administration-of -information-in-Higher-Education- Role-of-ICT

Clark, T. (2001).*Virtual schools: Trends and issues*. Phoenix, AZ: WestEd/Distance Learning ResourceNetwork.

Collins, S. (2004). U.S. Department of Education white paper on e-Learning Frameworks for NCLB.Retrieved from http://www.nclbtechsummits.org/summit2/presentations/Collinse-LearningFramework.pdf

Collins, A. (1996). "Design issues for learning environments". *In S. Vosniadou (Ed.), International perspectives on the design of technology-supported learning environments* (Pp. 347–361). Mahwah, NJ: Lawrence Erlbaum.

Goshit, T. (2006). Nigeria's need for ICT: SP. 259 technology and policy in Africa. Available: http://ocw.mit.edu/NR/rdonlyres/Special-Programs/SP-259Spring-2006/891209EE-E63B-4617-BA9D-7635A63C754B/0/goshit.pdf

Gronow, M. (2007).*ICT Leadership in School Education;* A Paper presented to the Australian Catholic University Conference. The Sofitel Wentworth, Sydney, Australia.

Esoswo, F. O (2011) Issues and challenges in the use of information Communication technology (icts) in education

Evoh, C.J. (2007) Policy networks and the transformation of secondary education Through ICTs in Africa: The prospects and challenges of the NEPAD E-schools Initiative. *International Journal of Education andDevelopment Using Information and Communication echnology (IJEDICT)* 3 (1), 64-84. Available:http://ijedict.dec.uwi.edu/include/getdoc. php?id=2198&article=272&mode=pdf

Flecknoe, M. (2002)."How can ICT help us to improve education"? *Innovations in Education & Teaching International,* **Vol.** 39, No. 4, Pp; 271-280

Girasoli, A. J. &Hannafin, R. D. (2008). "Using asynchronous AV communication tools to increase academic self-efficacy". *Computers & Education,* **Vol.** 51 No. (4), Pp; 1676- 1682.

Grey, C.J. (2005). Knowledge management practices for sustainable construction: *Political tensions in engineering ICT knowledge tools in the private and public sectors, Information, Knowledge and Management*: re-assessing the role of ICTs in public and private organizations, Rome Superior School of Public Administration, ESRC, the University of Manchester, UMIST and the University of Pisa,

Hasan (2007). CIT reflections, Annual Magazine of the FTK-Centre for Information Technology,JamiaMilliaIslamia, New Delhi, Issue-1 April 2007.

Iloanusi, NO. &Osuagwu, C.C. (2010).An evaluation of the impact of ICT diffusion in Nigeria's higher educational system.*Journal of Information Technology Impact,* 10(1), 25-34.

Iwu, A.O. & Ike, G.A. (2009).Information and Communication Technology and Programme Instruction for the Attainment of Educational Goals in Nigeria's Secondary Schools. *Journal of the Nigeria Association for Educational Media and Technology (1)* September, 2009.

Jacinta, S.M (2014) Application of Information Communication Technology in School Administration in Public Secondary Schools in Lang'ata Division, Nairobi County, Kenya

JNT Association (2007).Introduction to Video Conferencing. *http://www.ja.net/vtas* © The JNT Association.

Jonassen, D. H., Peck, K. L., & Wilson, B. G. (1999).Learning with technology: *A constructivist perspective.* Upper Saddle River, NJ: Merrill.

Jonassen, D. & Reeves, T. (1996). Learning with technology: Using computers as cognitive tools. In D. Jonassen (Ed.), *Handbook of Research Educational on Educational Communications and Technology* (pp 693-719). New York: Macmillan.

Kennewell, S., Parkinson, J., & Tanner, H.(2000)."Developing the ICT capable school". London: Routledge Falmer.

Kozma, R.(2005), 'National Policies That Connect ICT-Based Education Reform To Economic And Social Development', *Human Technology* **Vol.**1, No. (2), Pp; 117-156.

Kulik, J. (2003). "Effects of using instructional technology in elementary and secondary schools: What controlled evaluation studies say (Final Report No.P10446.001)". *Arlington, VA: SRI International.*

Krishnaveni, R., &Meenakumari, J. (2010).Usage of ICT for Information Administration in Highereducation Institutions–A study.*International Journal of Environmental Science and Development,1*(3). Retrieved from http://www.ijesd.org/papers/55-D461.pdf

Liverpool, E.O .& Jacinta, A.O. (2013). Information and Communication Technologies (ICT): A Panacea to Achieving Effective Goals in Institutional Administration. *Middle-East Journal of Scientific research 18(9)*: 1380-1384. Retrieved on January 12, 2015 at: http://www.idosi.org/mejsr/mejsr18(9)13/22.pdf.

Lynne, D. (2007). Video Conferencing in Higher Education", *Institute of Computer Based Learning*, Heriot Watt University Edinburgh.

Lim, C. P. and Tay, Y. (2003). Information and communication technologies (ICT) in an elementary school: Students' engagement in higher-order thinking. *Journal of Educational Multimedia and Hypermedia*, 12(4), pp. 425–451.

Lim, C. P. &Chai, C.S. (2004), An activity-theoretical approach to research of ICT integration in Singapore schools: Orienting activities and learner autonomy', *Computers & Education* **Vol.** 43, No. (3), Pp; 215--236.

Long, S. (2001), "Multimedia in the art curriculum: Crossing boundaries". *Journal of Art and Design Education,* **Vol.**20, No.(3), Pp255-263.

Loveless, A. (2003), "Making a difference? An evaluation of professional knowledge and pedagogy in art and ICT".

Journal of Art and Design Education, **Vol.** 22, No. (2), Pp145154,

Magni (2009),"ICT usage in Higher education", International Technology and Education and Development Conference, Spain March 9-11 2009.

Mason, R. (2000), 'From distance education to online education', *The Internet and Higher Education* **Vol** .3No.(1-2),Pp; 63-74.

McGorry, S. Y. (2002), 'Online, but on target? Internet-based MBA courses: A case study', *The Internet and Higher Education* **Vol.**5, No. (2), Pp; 167-175.

Mevarech, A. R., & Light, P. H. (1992). Peer-based interaction at the computer: Looking backward, looking forward. *Learning and Instruction*, **Vol.**2, Pp; 275-280.

Mooij, T. (1999).Guidelines to Pedagogical Use of ICT in Education. Paper presented at the 8th Conference of the '*European Association for Research on Learning and Instruction*' (EARLI). Goteborg, Sweden, August 1999.

Mooij, T. (2007), 'Design of educational and ICT conditions to integrate differences in learning: Contextual learning theory and a first transformation step in early education', *Computers in Human Behaviour* **Vol.** 23, No. (3), Pp; 1499--1530.

Moore, M. &Kearsley, G. (1996). Distance Education: A Systems View. Belmont, CA: Wadsworth. New Media Consortium (2007)."Horizon Report, retrieved July 1, 2007 from *www.nmc. org/pdf/2007_Horizon_Report.pdf.*

Mueen,U. Asadullah, S., Raed, A.&Jamshed, M. (2013). Measuring Efficiency of Tier Level data Centers, *Middle-East Journal of Scientific Research, 15(2)*: 200-207.

MacDougall, A. & Squires, D. (1997). A framework for reviewing professional development programmes in information technology. *Journal of Information Technology,* 115-126.

McInnis, C. (2004). *Studies of Student Life: an overview.* European Journal of Education,Vol. 39, No. 4, 2004.

Myers, J. M., Halpin, R. (2002). Teachers' attitudes and use of multimediatechnology in the classroom: constructive-based professional developmenttraining for school districts. *Journal of Computing in Teacher Education* 18(4) 133 – 140.

Nakpodia, E. D. (2011). Students' records: Challenges in the management of student personnel in Nigeria tertiary institutions. *Prime Journals, 1*(3), 44-49.

NASPA- Student Affairs Administrators in Higher Education (2012) Considering a Career in Student Affairs? Retrieved from<u>http://www.naspa.org/career/default.cfm</u>

Oboegbulem, A., &Ugwu, R. N. (2013).*The Place of ICT (Information and Communication Technology) in the Administration of Secondary Schools in South Eastern States of Nigeria, 3*(4),231-38.Retrievedfromhttp://www.eric.ed.gov/?q

Oduroye, A.P. (n.d.) Challenges of learning and teaching with computers. Available: http://www.itnetwork.org.uk/56.htm

Opara, J., &Onyije, L. (2014). Information and Communication Technologies (ICT): A panacea toachieving effective goals in institutional administration. *International Letters of Social and Humanistic Sciences, 1,* 81-87. http://dx.doi.org/10.5901/mjss.2013.v4n13p227

Ohakwe, S. &Okwuanaso, S. (2006). The access centre: improving outcomes for all Students K-8 Department of Education Programme Office of Special Education. Programmes Washington DC.

Okebukola, P. (2004). E-learning in varsities, others underway, NUC boss lists strategies. *The Guardian* (12 October): 35, 39.

Olisaemeka, B. U., Onwusoanya, B. U. (2009). *Lecturers' attitude towards theuse of computer inventions: a Nigerian case.* Paper presented at the National Conference of the Nigeria Association of Educational Administration andPlanning (NAEAP) at the Women Development Centre, Akwa, AnambraState, Nigeria. 21 -25 September.

Osakwe, R. (2012). Problems and Prospects of Using Information and Communication Technology for Record Keeping in Tertiary Institutions in Nigeria.*Journal of Education and Practice*, 39-43.

PasaMemisoglu, S. (2007). The supervision of information technology classrooms in Turkey: A nationwide survey. *Australasian Journal of Educational Technology, 23*(4), 529-541.

Pelgrum, W. J., Law, N. (2003) "ICT in Education around the World: Trends, Problems and Prospects"UNESCO-*International Institute for Educational Planning.* Available:

www.worldcatlibraries.org/wcpa/ow/02d077080fcf3210a19a
feb4da09e526.html.

Plomp, T.; Pelgrum, W. J. & Law, N. (2007), 'SITES2006—
International comparative survey of pedagogical practices
and ICT in education', *Education and Information
Technologies* **Vol.**12, No. (2), Pp; 83- 92.

Roberts, R. (2009). Video Conferencing in Distance Learning:
A New Zealand School's Perspective. *Journal of Distance
Learning ©Distance Education Association of New Zealand,*
Vol. 13, pp. 91 – 107.

Rutherford, J. (2004). Technology in the schools.*Technology in
Society, 26,* 149-160.

Sanyal, B. C. (2001), 'New functions of higher education and ICT
to achieve education for all', Paper prepared for the Expert
Roundtable on University and Technology-for- Literacy
and Education Partnership in Developing Countries,
International Institute for Educational Planning, UNESCO,
September 10 to 12, Paris.

Sharma, R. (2003), 'Barriers in Using Technology for Education
in Developing Countries', IEEE0-7803-7724-9103.Singapore
schools', *Computers & Education* **Vol** .41, No.(1),Pp; 49--63.

Sami, A. (2008). Post Graduate Thesis: Video Conferencing
in Distance Learning. *Department of Computer Science,*
University of Helsinki.

Smeets, E., Mooij, T., Bamps, H., Bartolom, A., Lowyck, J.,
Redmond, D., & Steffens, K. (1999).The Impact of Information

and Communication Technology on the Teacher. Nijmegen, the Netherlands: University of Nijmegen, ITS. *webdoc.ubn. kun.nl/anon/i/impaofina.pdf [February 15, 2004]*.

Thomas, K,O. (2004), "Practical Application Of ICT To Enhance University Education InGhana", Feature Article, Ghana Web 2004.

UNESCO-United Nations Educational, Scientific and Cultural Organization (2002). *The Role of Student Affairs and Services in HigherEducation: A Practical Manual for Developing, Implementing, and Assessing Student Affairs Programmes and Services.* Paris, UNESCO.Follow-up to the World Conference on Higher Education (Paris 5-9 October 1998)

UNESCO.(2012). A curriculum for secondary schools and programme for teachers' development.*Information and communication technology (ICT) in education* (pp. 104 - 126). Paris: UNESCO.

Visscher, A. J., Wild, P., & Fung, A. C. (2001).*Information Technology in Educational Management: Synthesis of Experience, Research and Future Perspectives on Computer-assisted School Information Systems.* The Netherlands: Kluwer Academic Publishers.

Webb, M., & Cox, M. (2004). A review of pedagogy related to information and communications technology. *Technology, Pedagogy and Education*, **Vol.** 13 No. (3), Pp; 235–286.

Yusuf, M.O. (2005). Information and communication education: Analyzing the Nigerian national policy forinformation technology. *International Education Journal 6* (3), 316-321.

Yuen, A.; Law, N. & Wong, K. (2003), 'ICT implementation and school leadership Case studies of ICT integration in teaching and learning', *Journal of Educational Administration* **Vol**. 41 No. 2, Pp;158-170.

Zapeda, S. J. (2007). *Instructional Supervision Applying Tools and Concepts.* Larchmont, NY: Eye on Education.

Printed in the United States
By Bookmasters